I dedicate *Color My Moods Adult Coloring Books and Journals* **Flower Mandalas and Patterns** to my family and to all the wonderful colorists who bring my artwork to life!

*— Maria Castro*

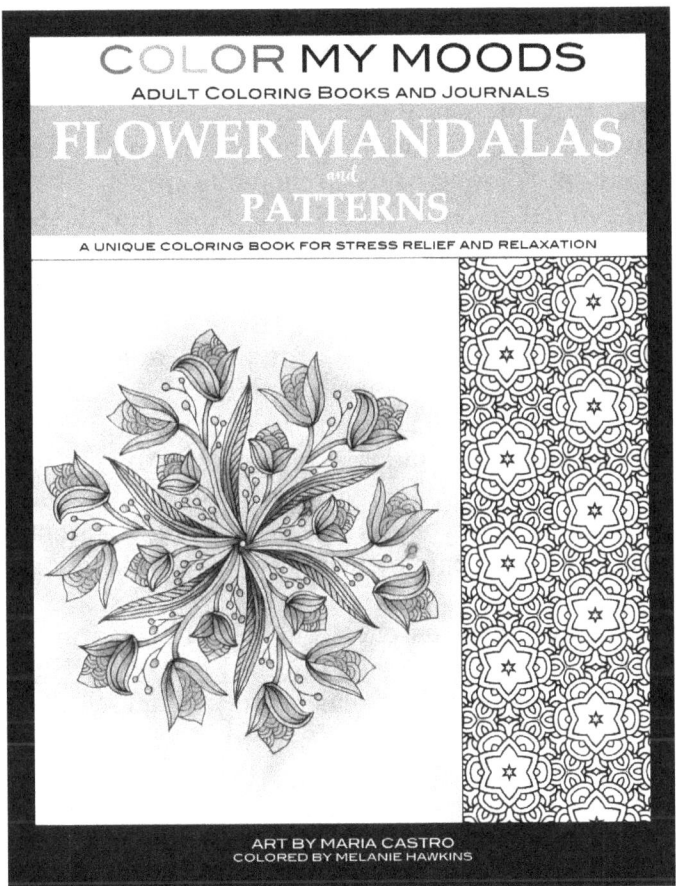

**Special thanks to:**

**Melanie Hawkins** *for the front cover coloring*

**Mara Lula** *for sharing her valuable feedback*

Thank you for adding *Color My Moods Adult Coloring Books and Journals* **Flower Mandalas and Patterns** to your adult coloring book collection! These original beautiful coloring pages from *Color My Moods* **Flower Mandalas and Patterns** will remind you of stepping into a glorious garden surrounded by gorgeous flowers. May coloring this book give you the same soothing and relaxing feelings.

I'm happy to share another unique adult coloring book with you, our coloring friends. Check out *Color My Moods* **Flower Mandalas and Patterns**:

- All original, stress-relieving mandala drawings and patterns ranging from simple to intricate to suit your coloring mood any day. No stock art is used here so you won't have to worry about finding duplicates in books that you may already have.
- Each volume has 20 mandalas and 20 patterns ranging from simple to intricate. Whatever your coloring mood is, you'll have 40 coloring pages to choose from.
- Single-sided (drawing is printed on one side of the page only and the back side is blank), 55# white coloring pages make it suitable for different media including colored pencils, markers, gel pens, pastels, crayons, and more. We recommend using the extra blank sheets provided as blotter pages to minimize bleed through.
- Each mandala drawing size may vary but each is printed as large as the page will accommodate without the binding getting in the way. Ample blank space at the top and bottom of each page can also be used to test media and color combinations.
- **Flower Mandalas and Patterns** are fun and relaxing to color. You can free your mind and release your creativity — there are no right or wrong colors. The symmetrical and repetitive nature of mandalas and patterns allow you to focus on coloring the art and lose yourself in the process, relieving stress, helping with pain management, or just having fun.

If you love **Flower Mandalas and Patterns**, check out our other coloring books and coloring journals on Amazon and other fine online retailers: https://www.scribocreative.com/products/. This will also have links to video previews so you can see all the drawings included in each of our books before you buy them.

While on the product pages, we hope that you'll take a minute to leave a review. As an independent publisher, we strive to give you a five-star experience with every purchase. If you would like to give us feedback directly, you can email info@scribocreative.com.

For more coloring inspiration, freebies and exclusive discounts, subscribe to our enews: https://www.scribocreative.com/enews/.

Post your colored pages on social media with **#scribocreative #colormymoods** and you might just get a surprise from us. To connect with us, visit: **https://www.scribocreative.com/about/**.

Have a good-MOOD coloring day, every day!

*Maria Castro of ScriboCreative.com*

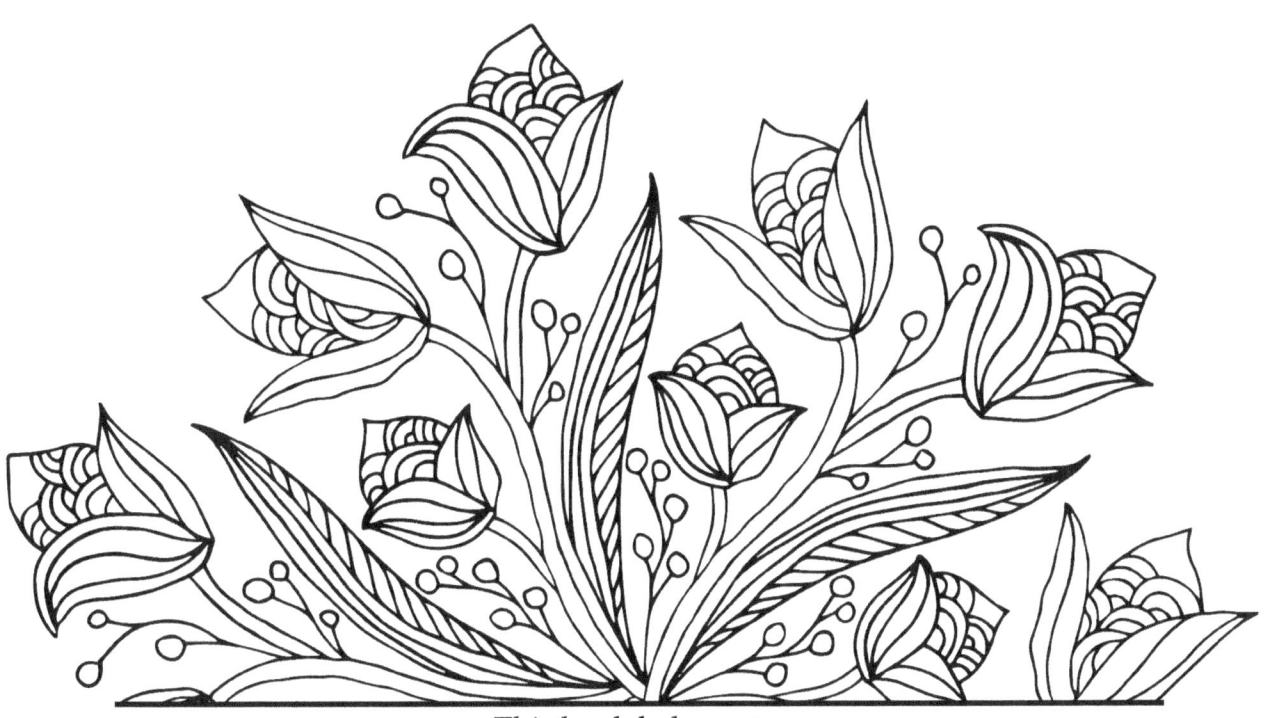

This book belongs to:

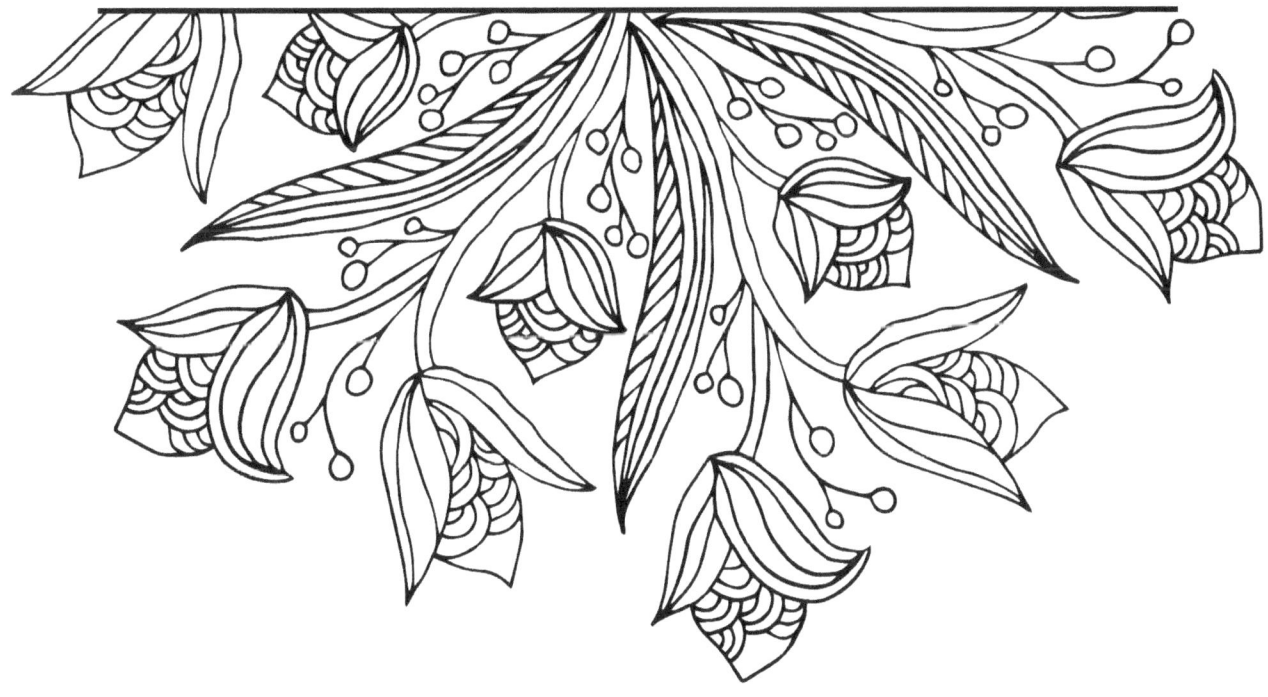

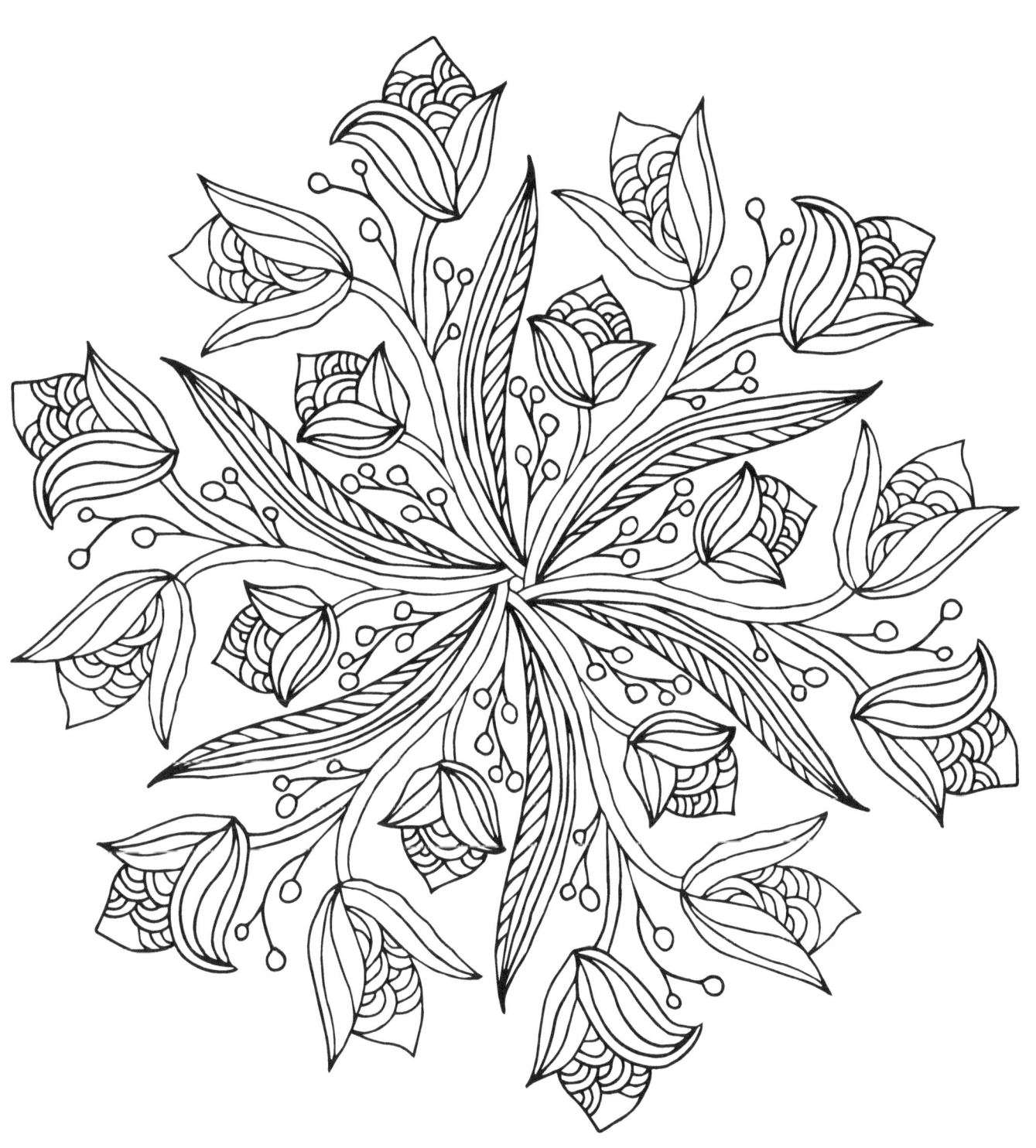

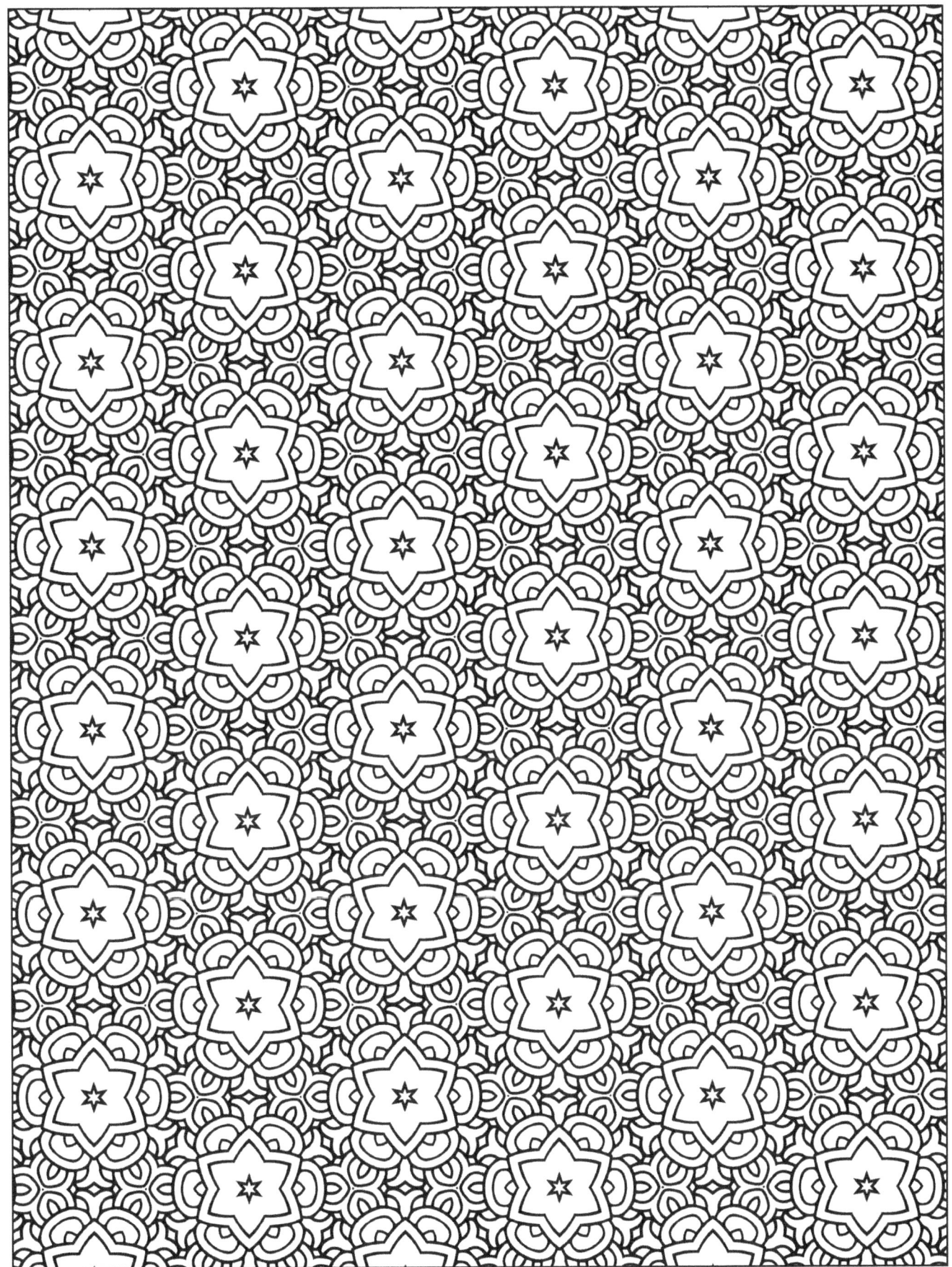

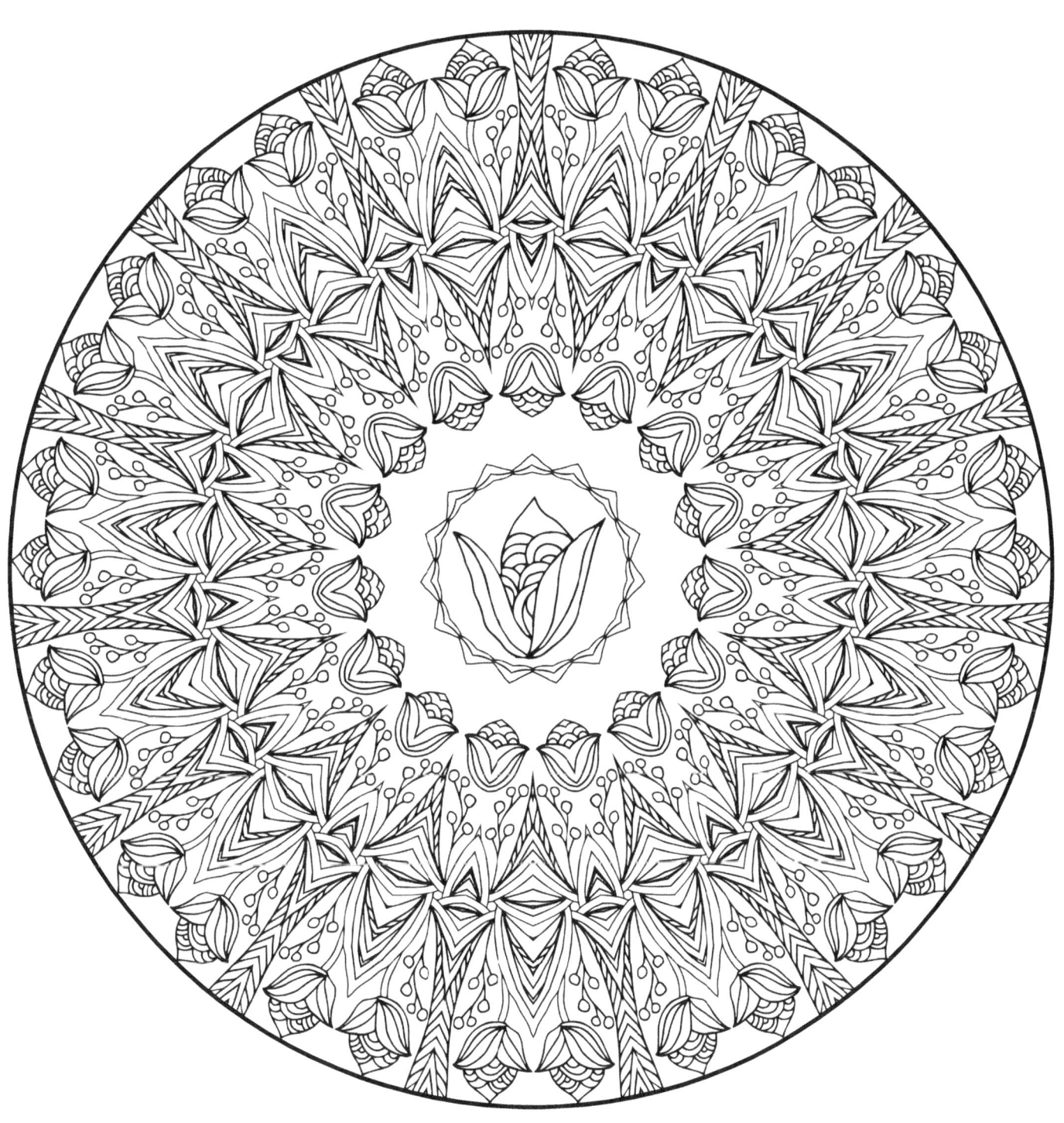

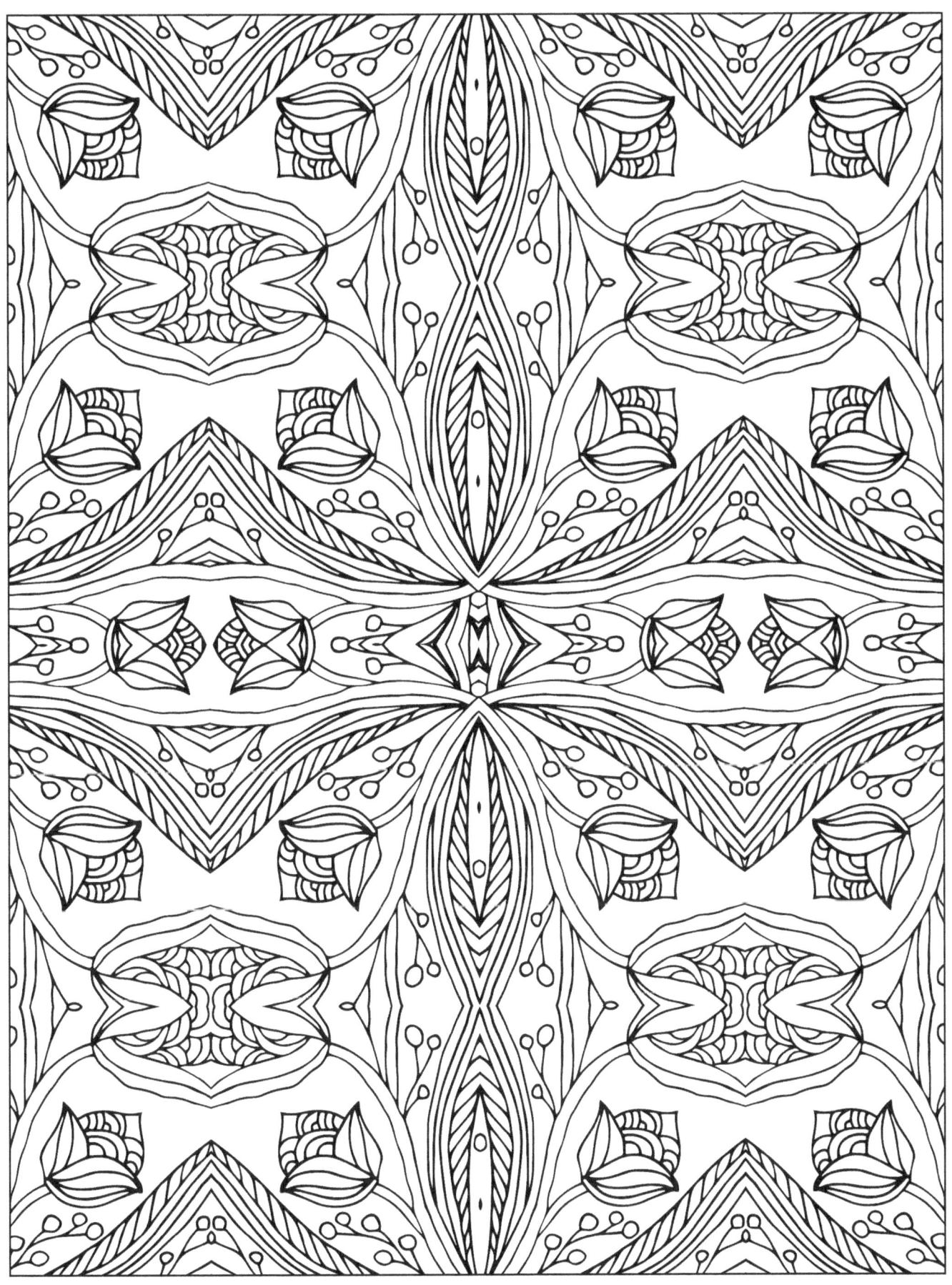

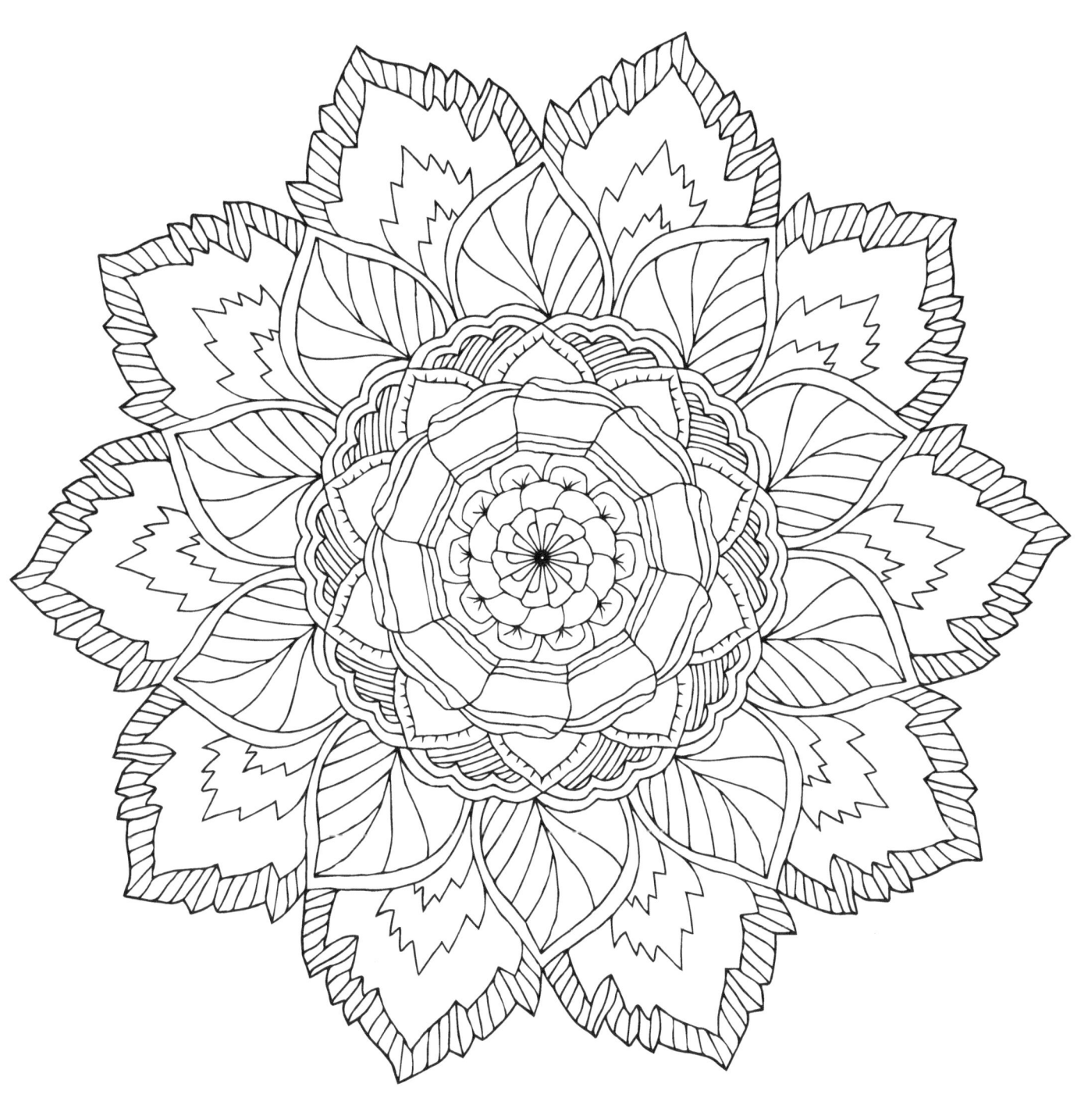

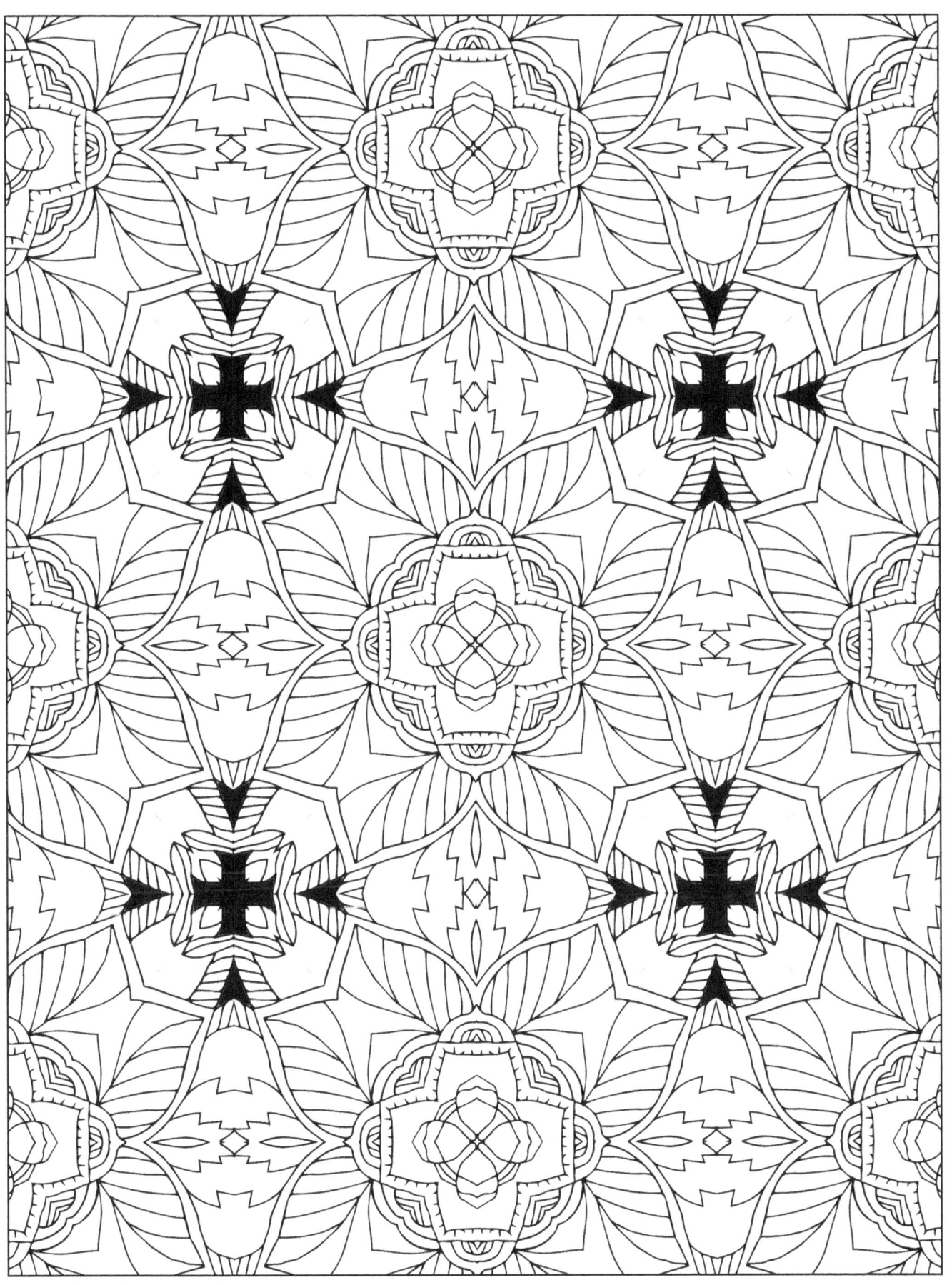

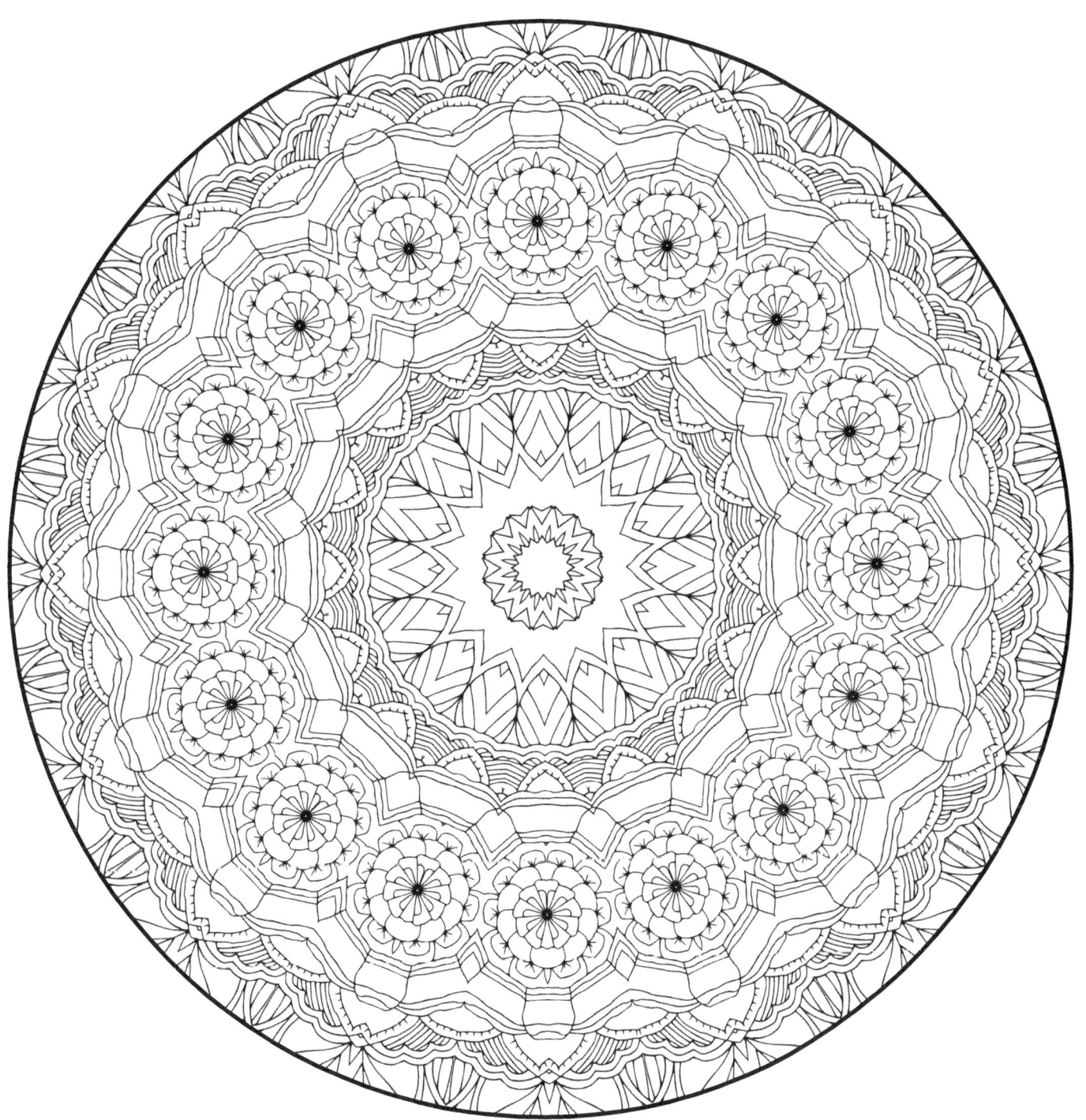

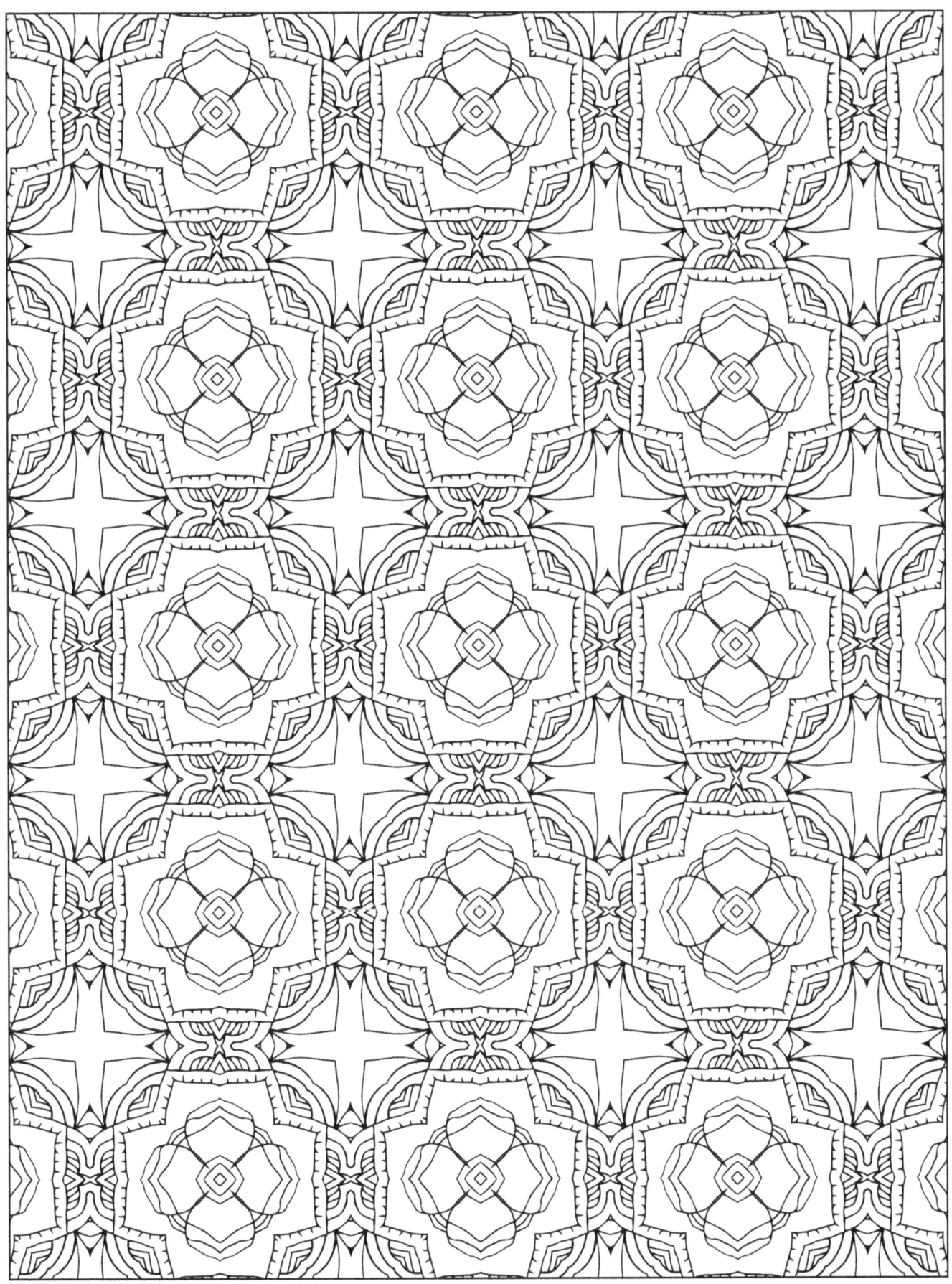

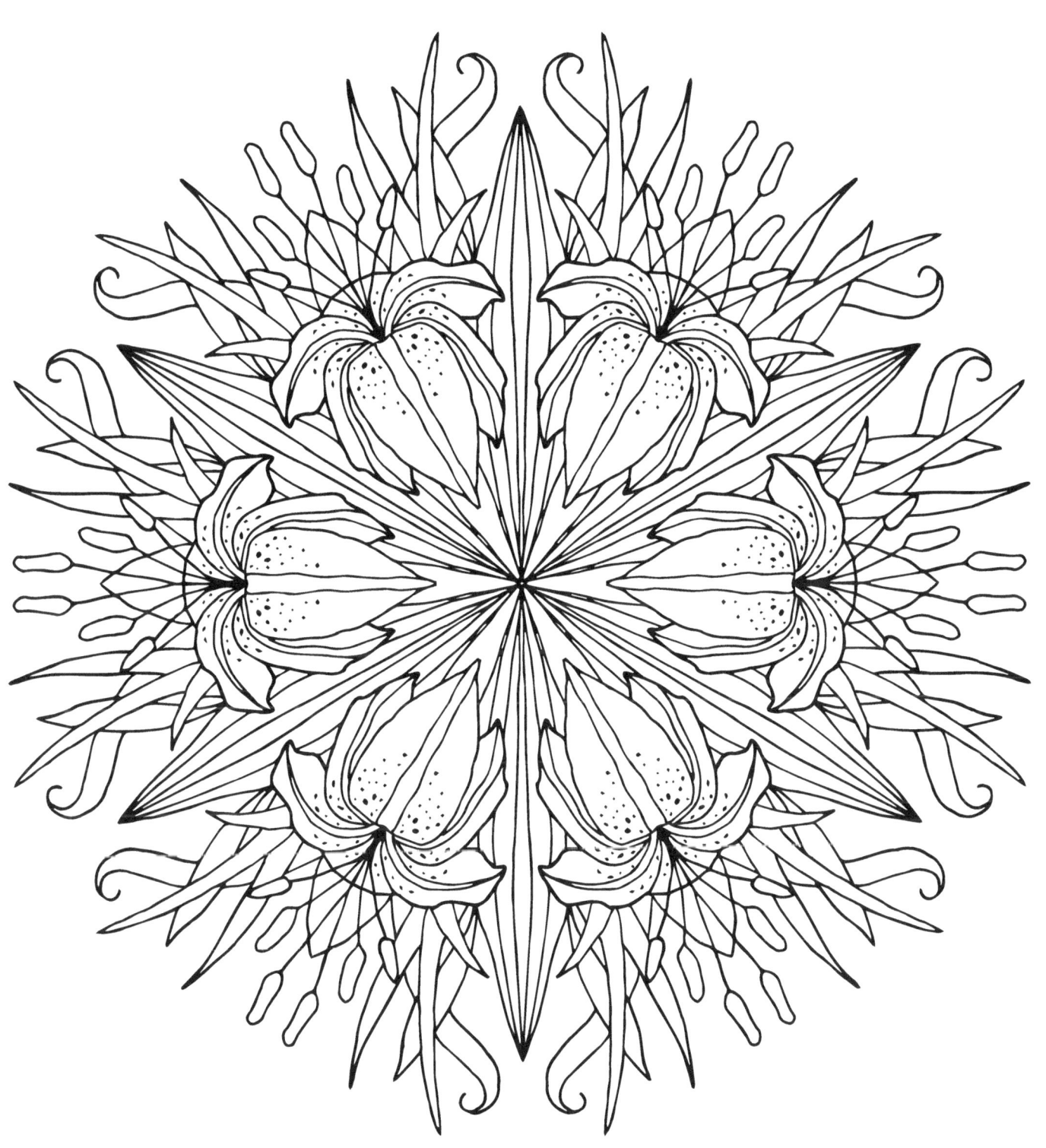

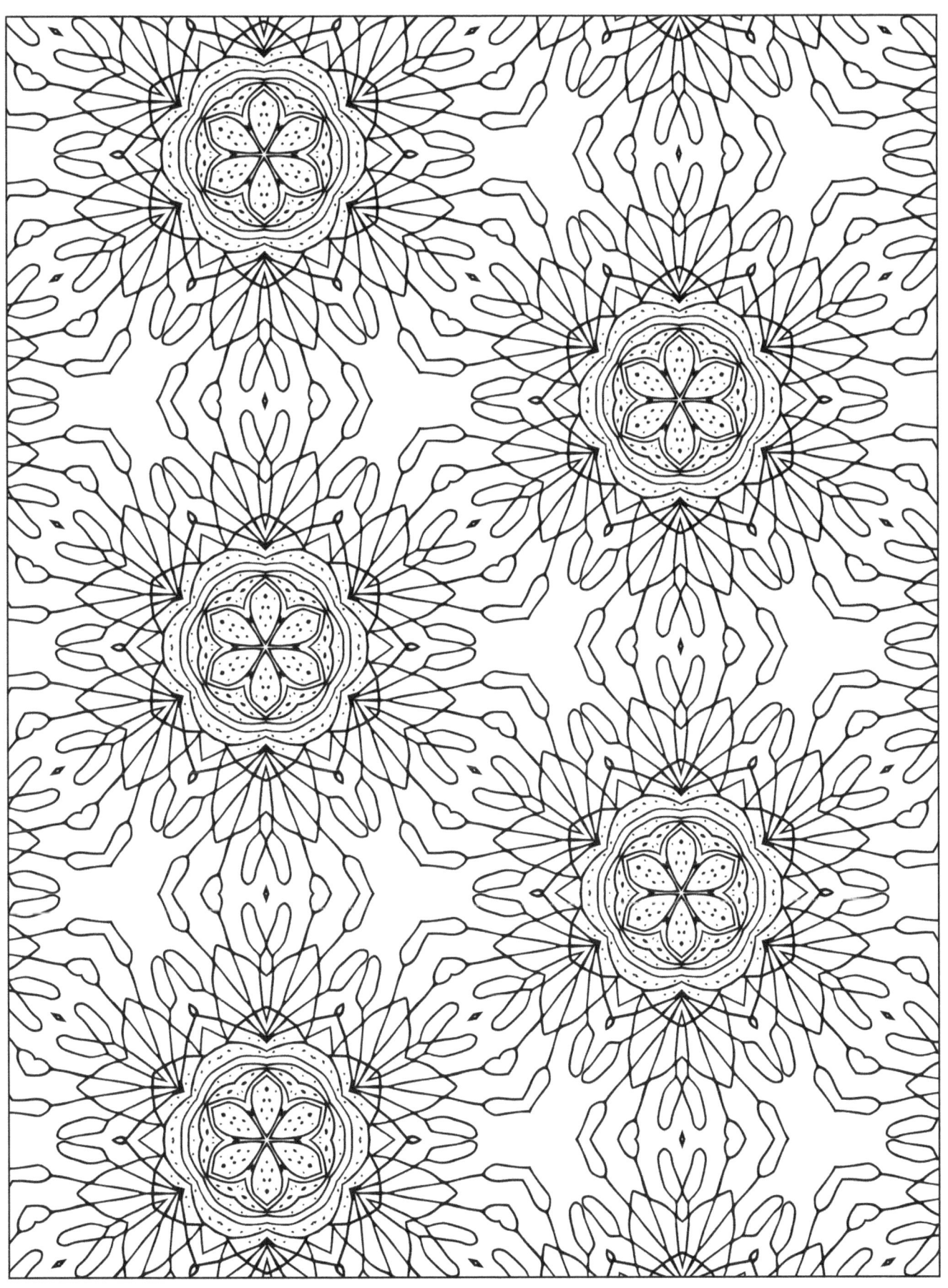

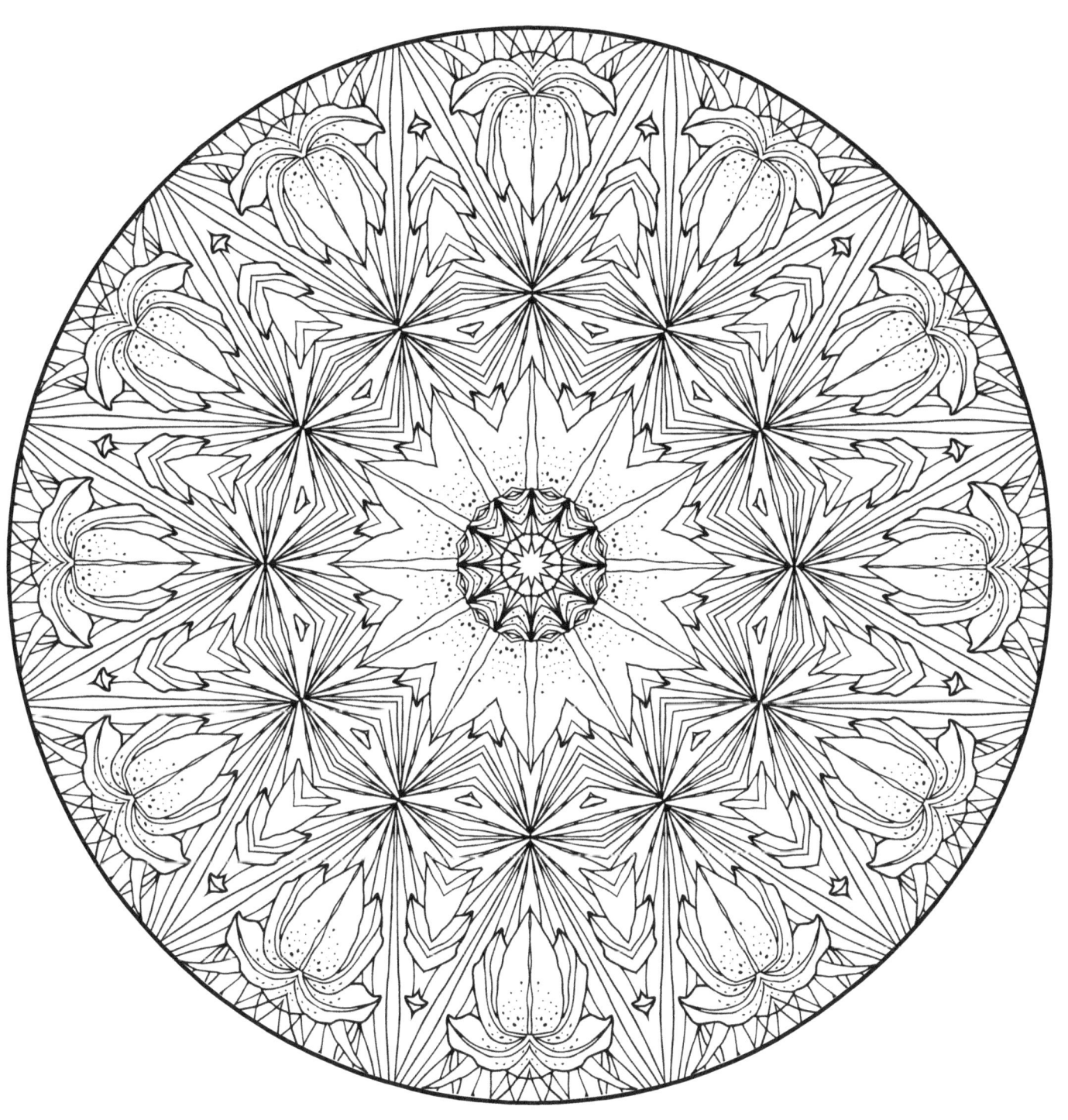

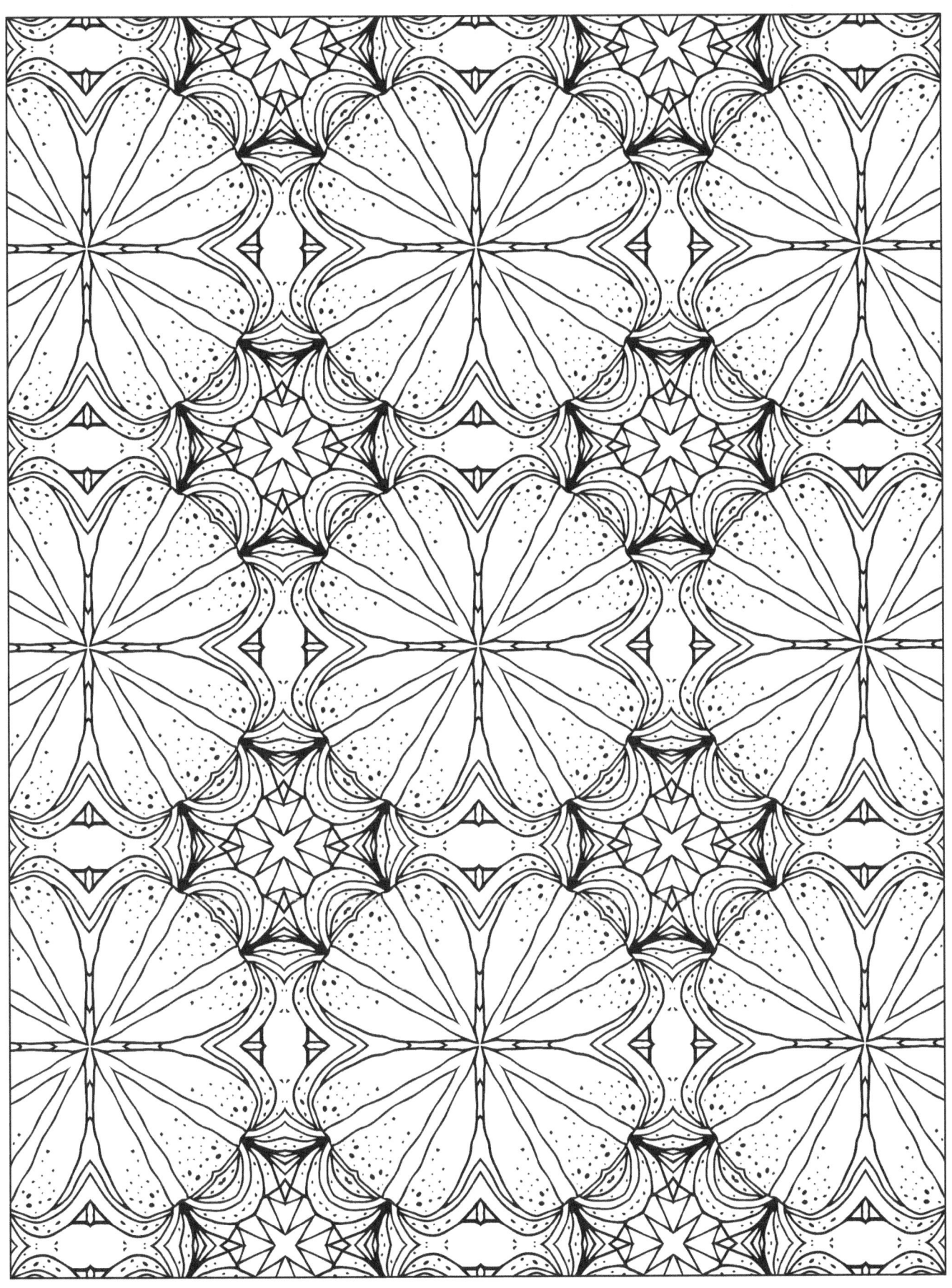

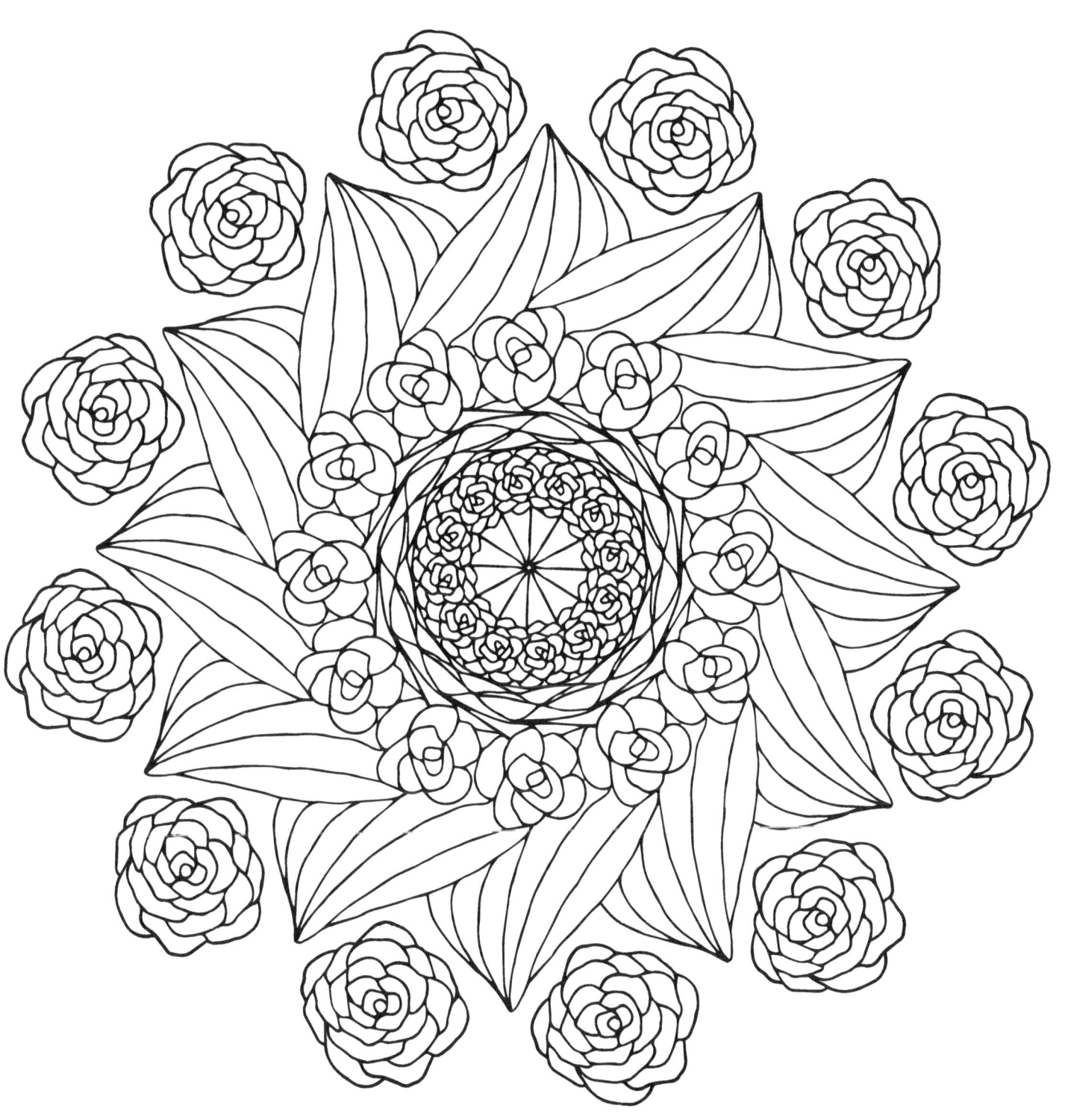

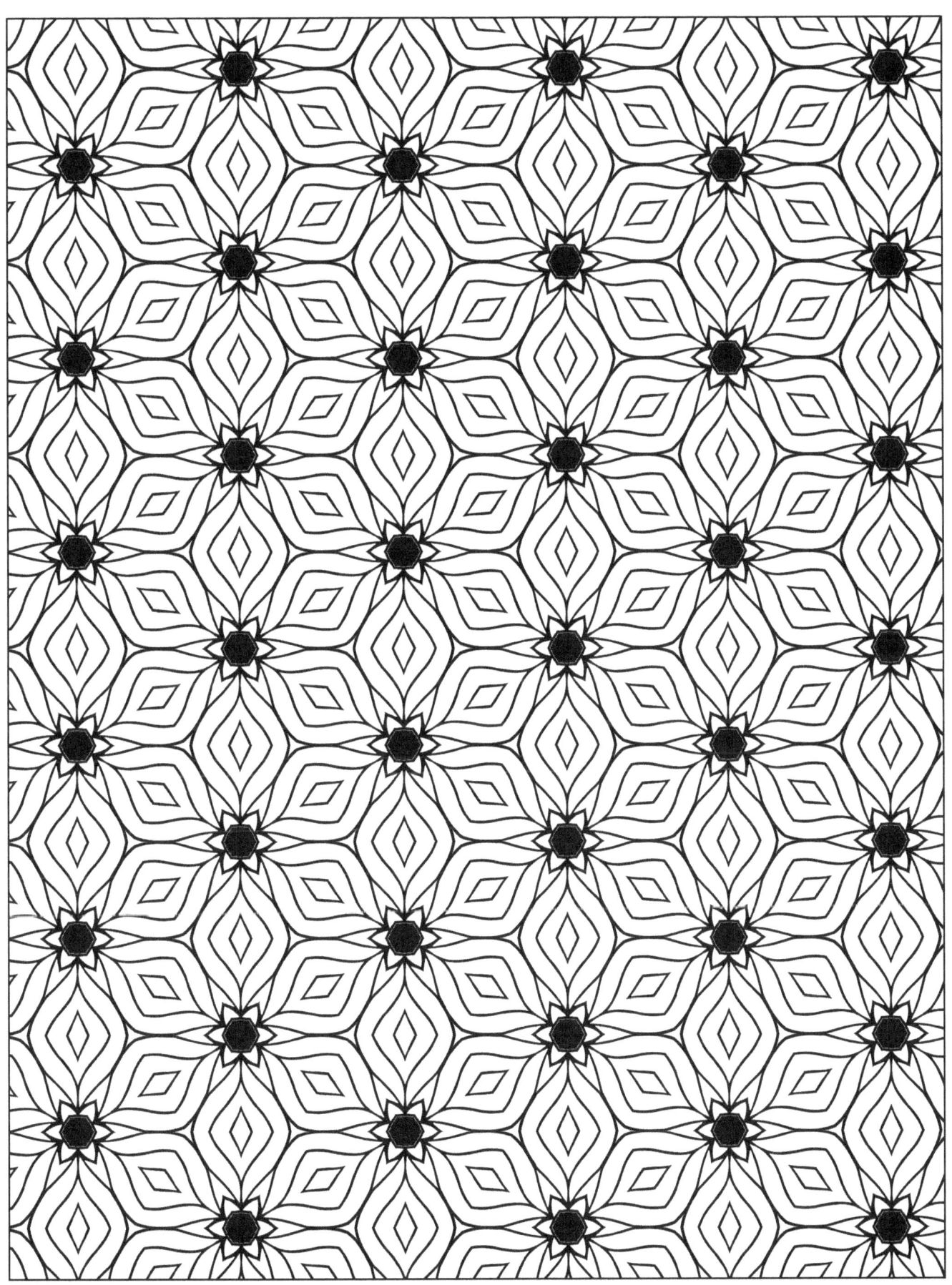

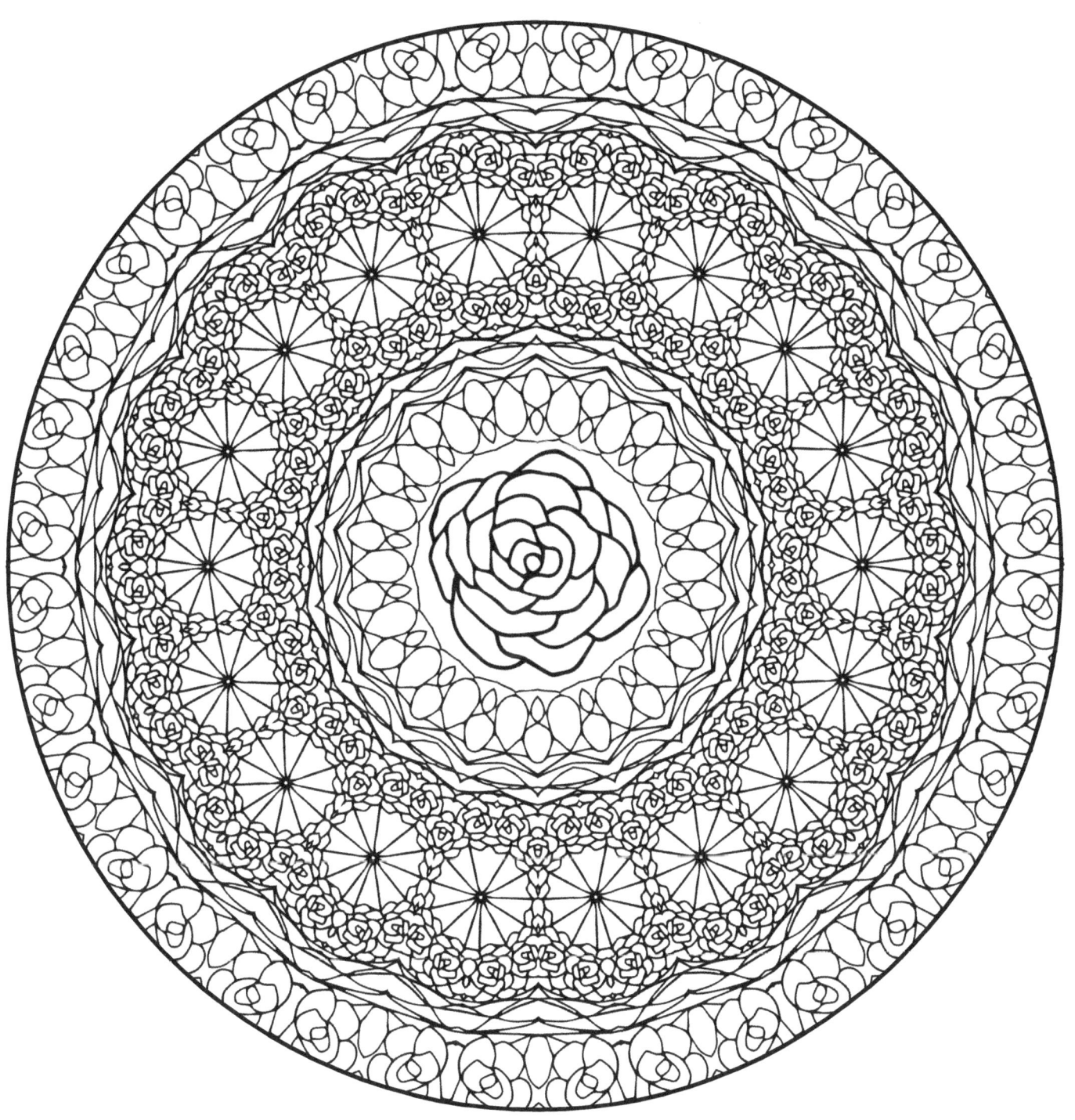

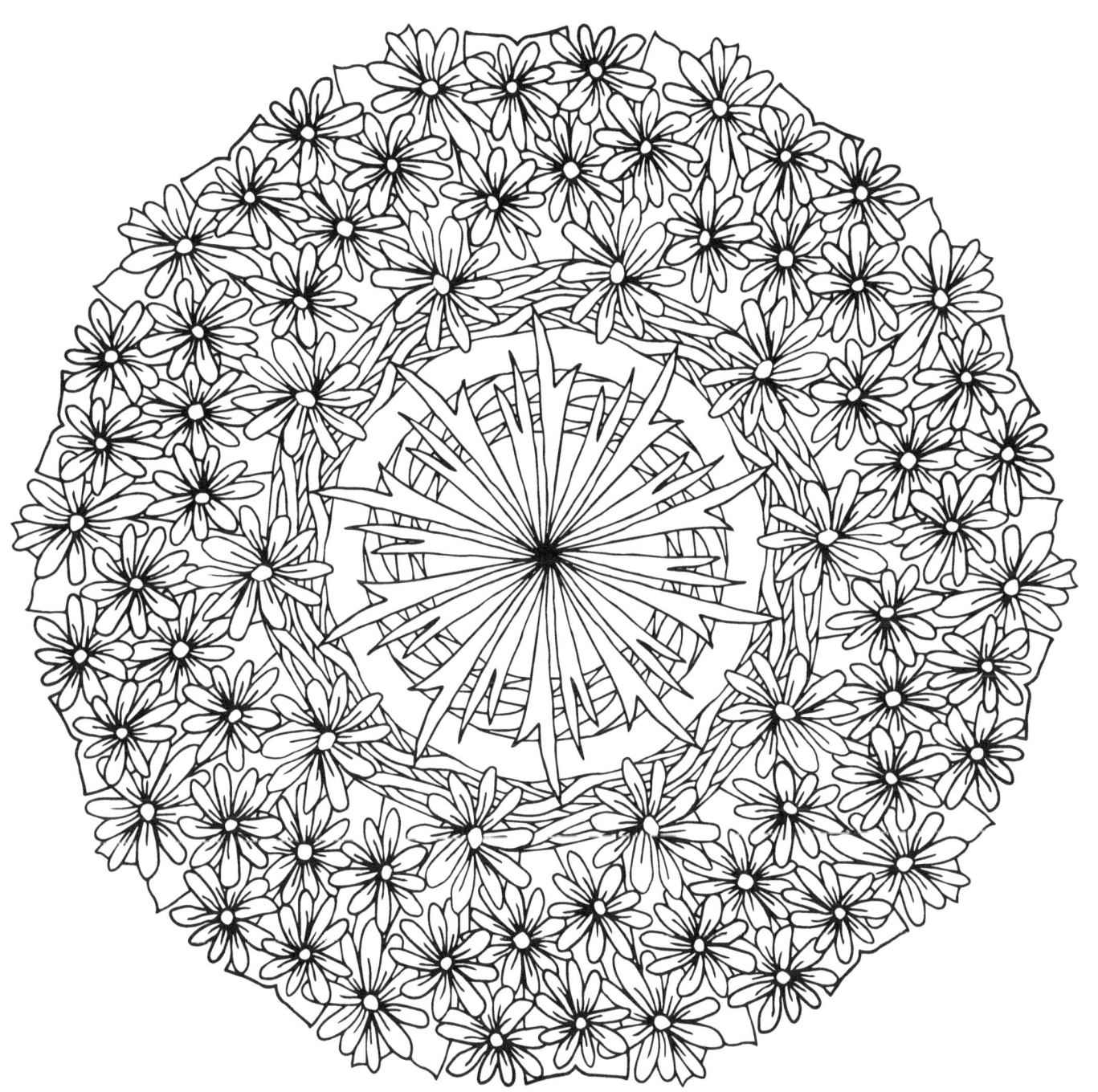

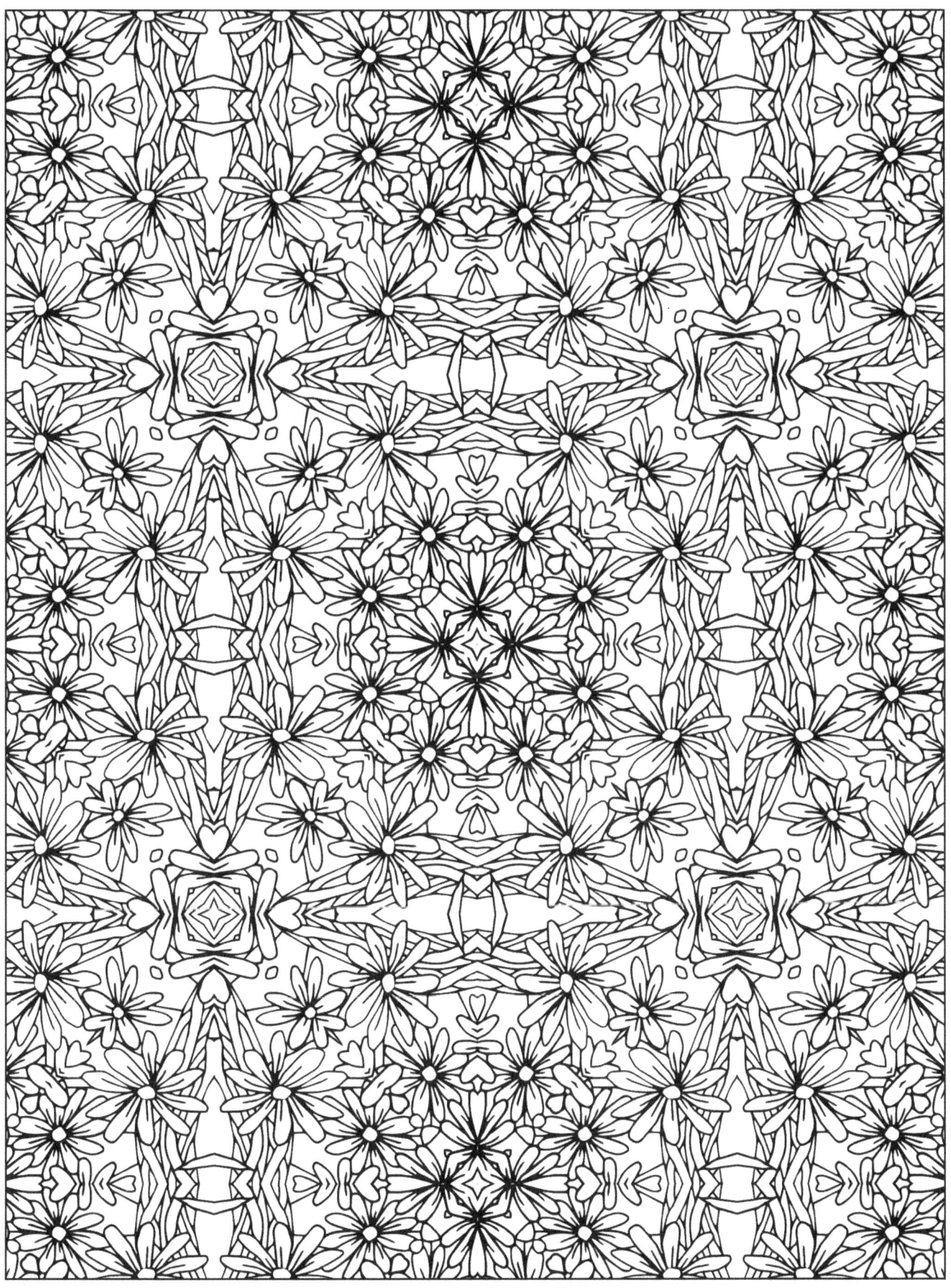

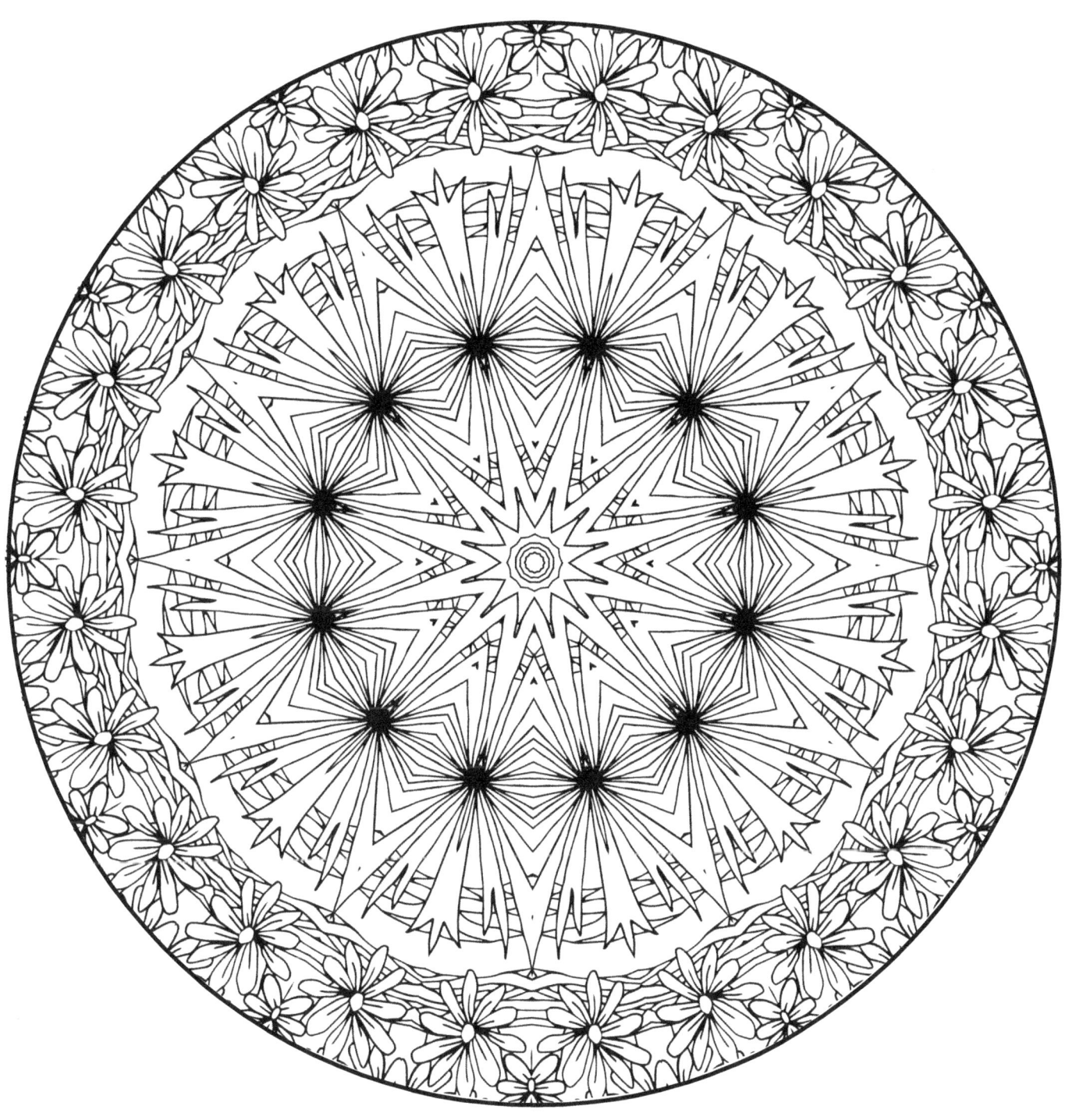

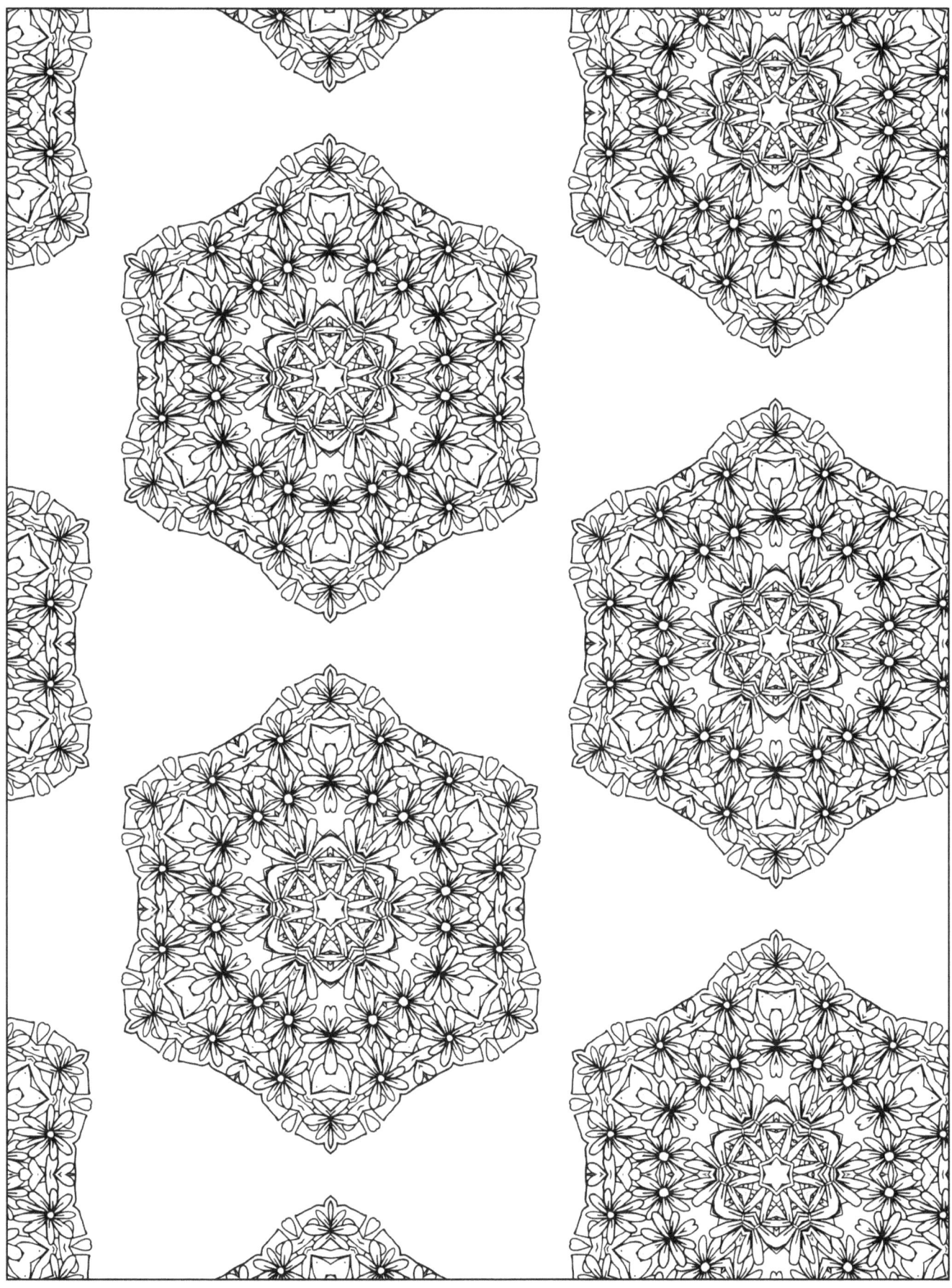

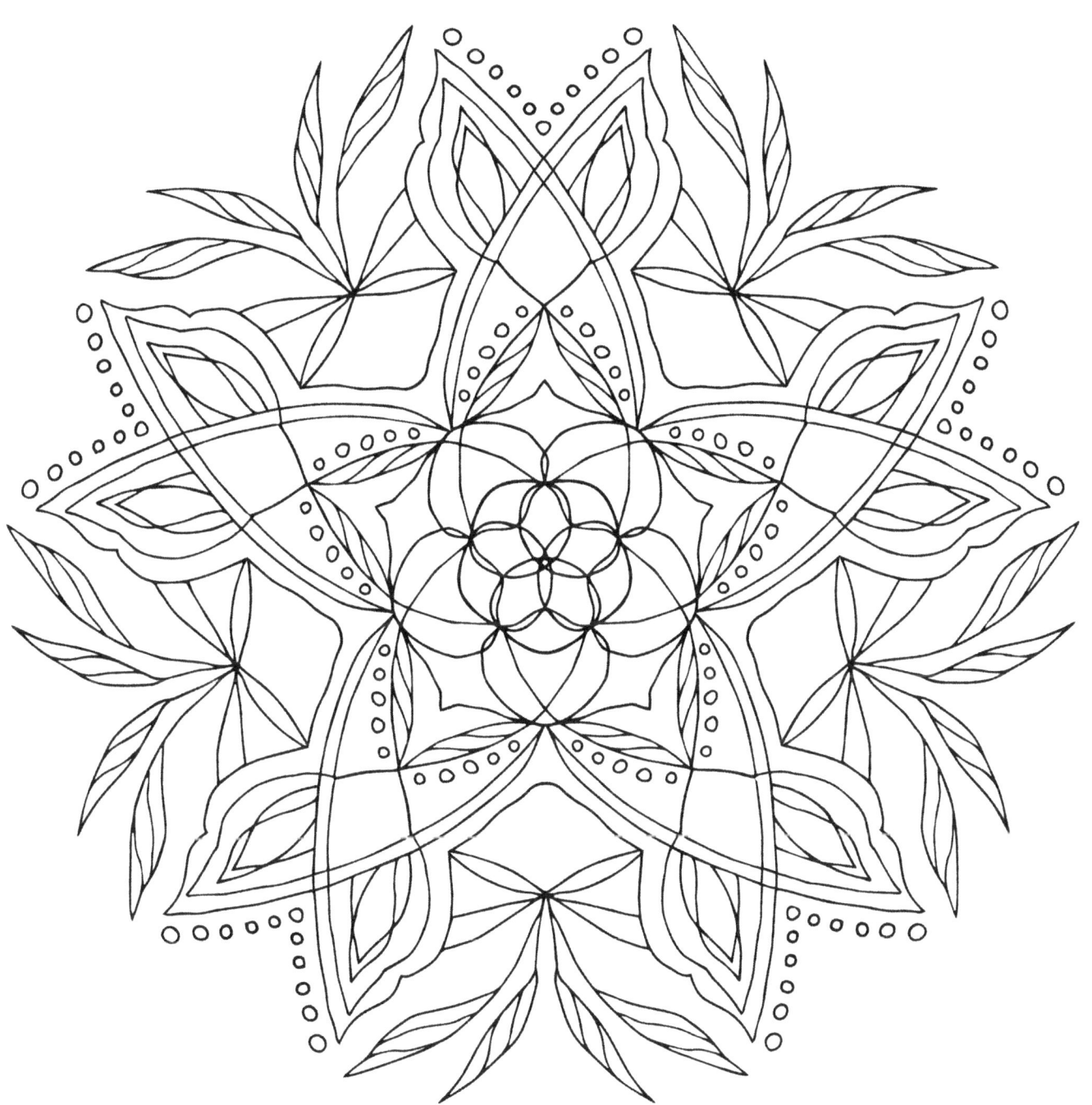

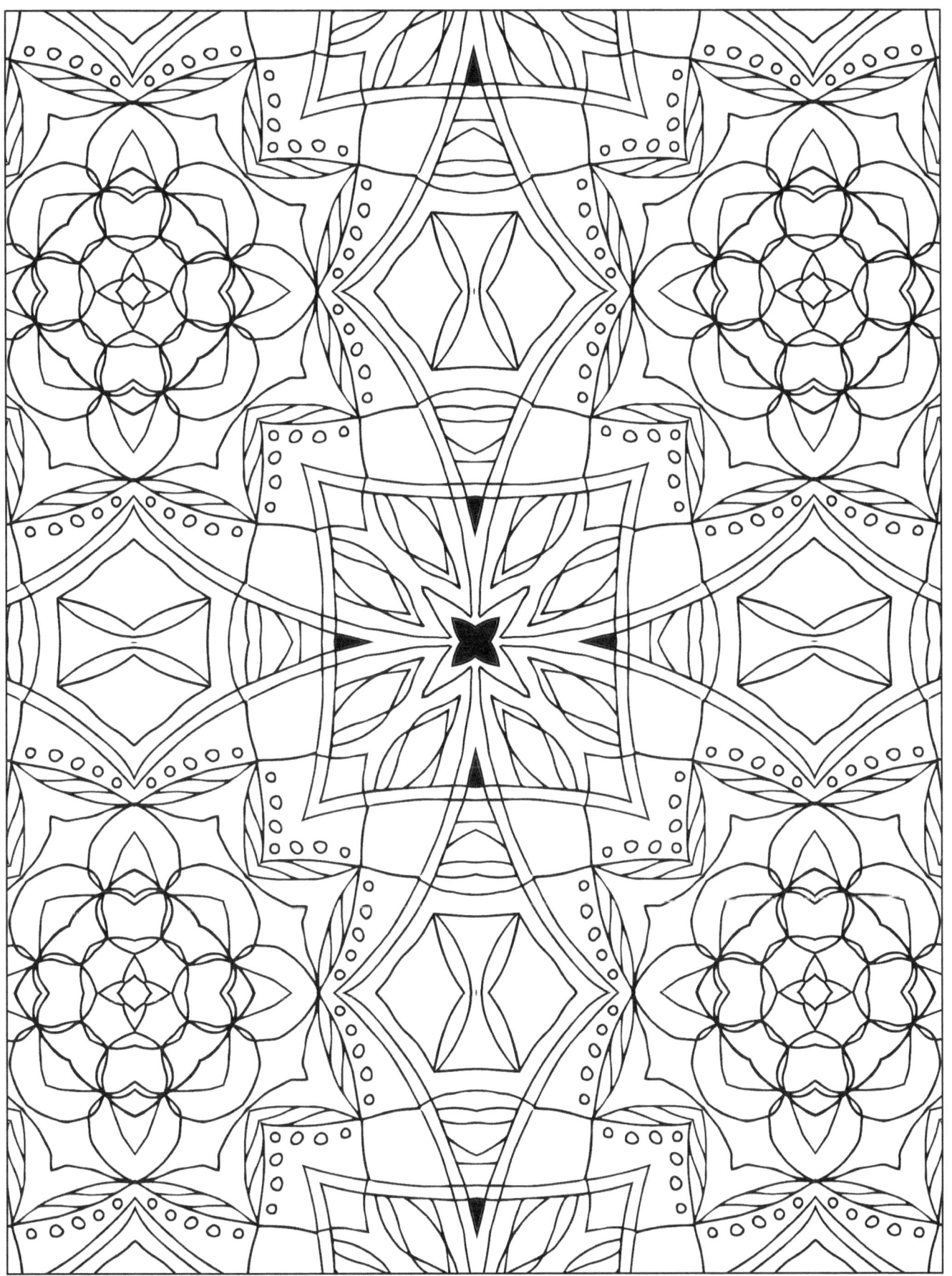

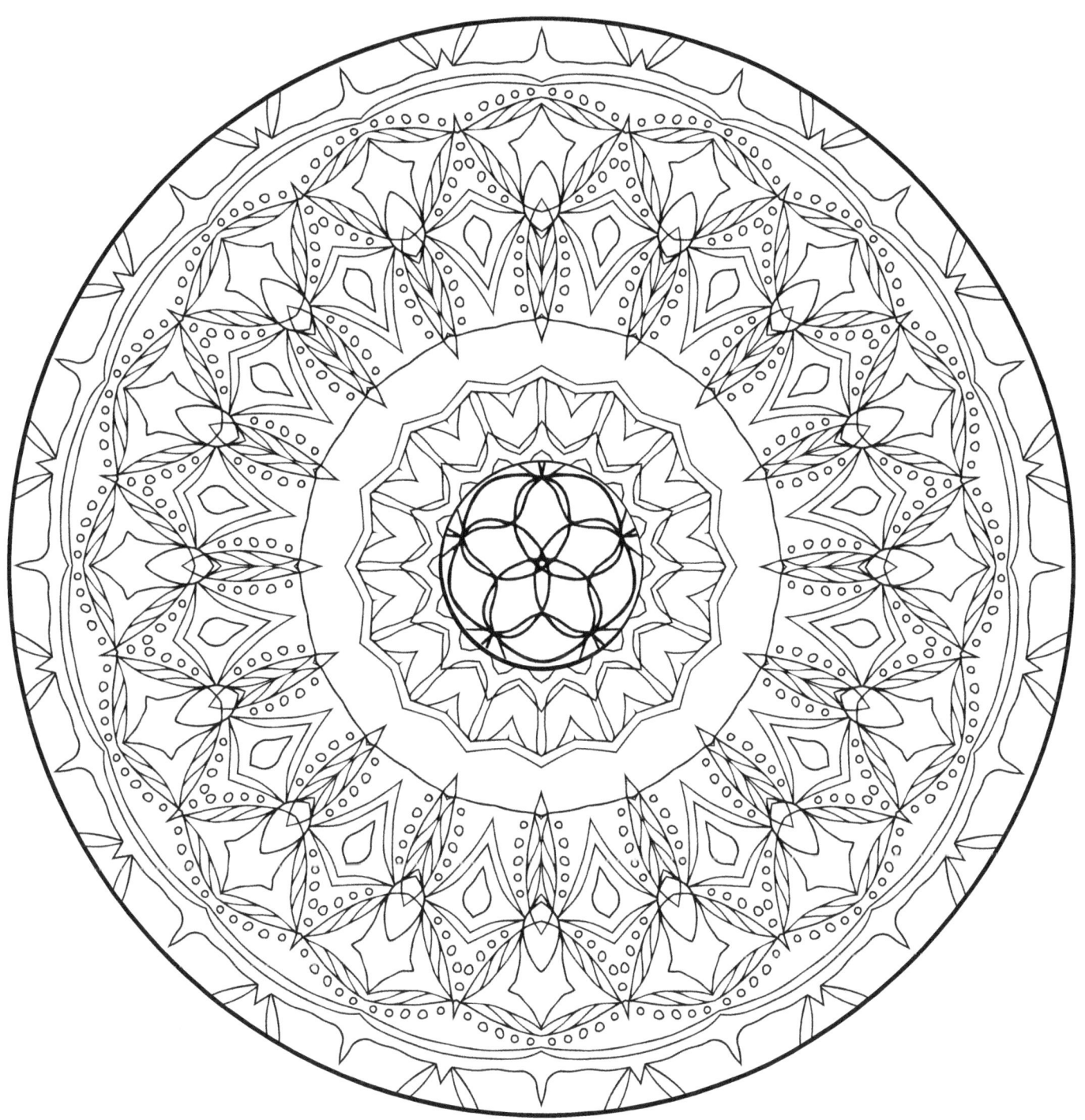

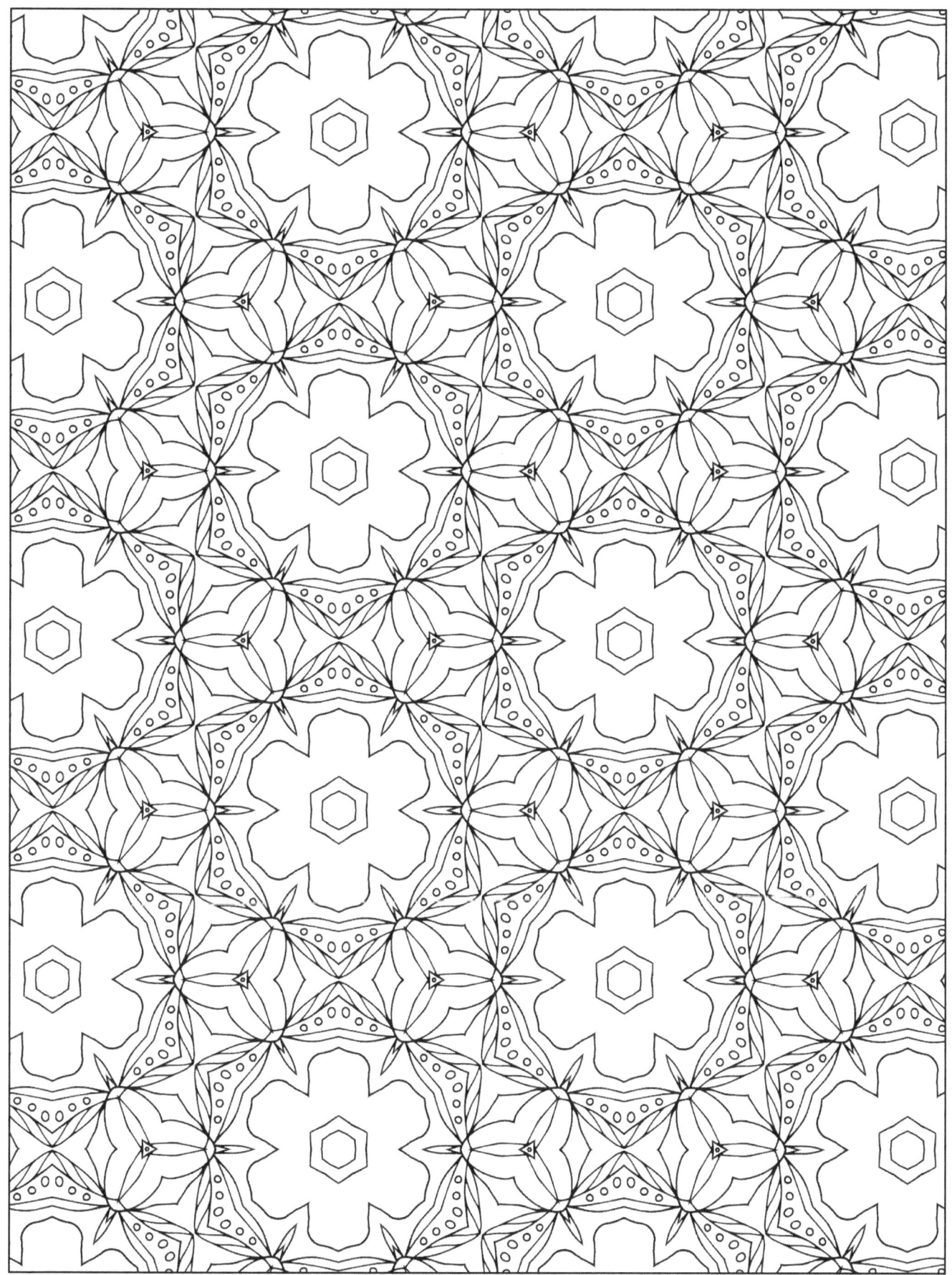

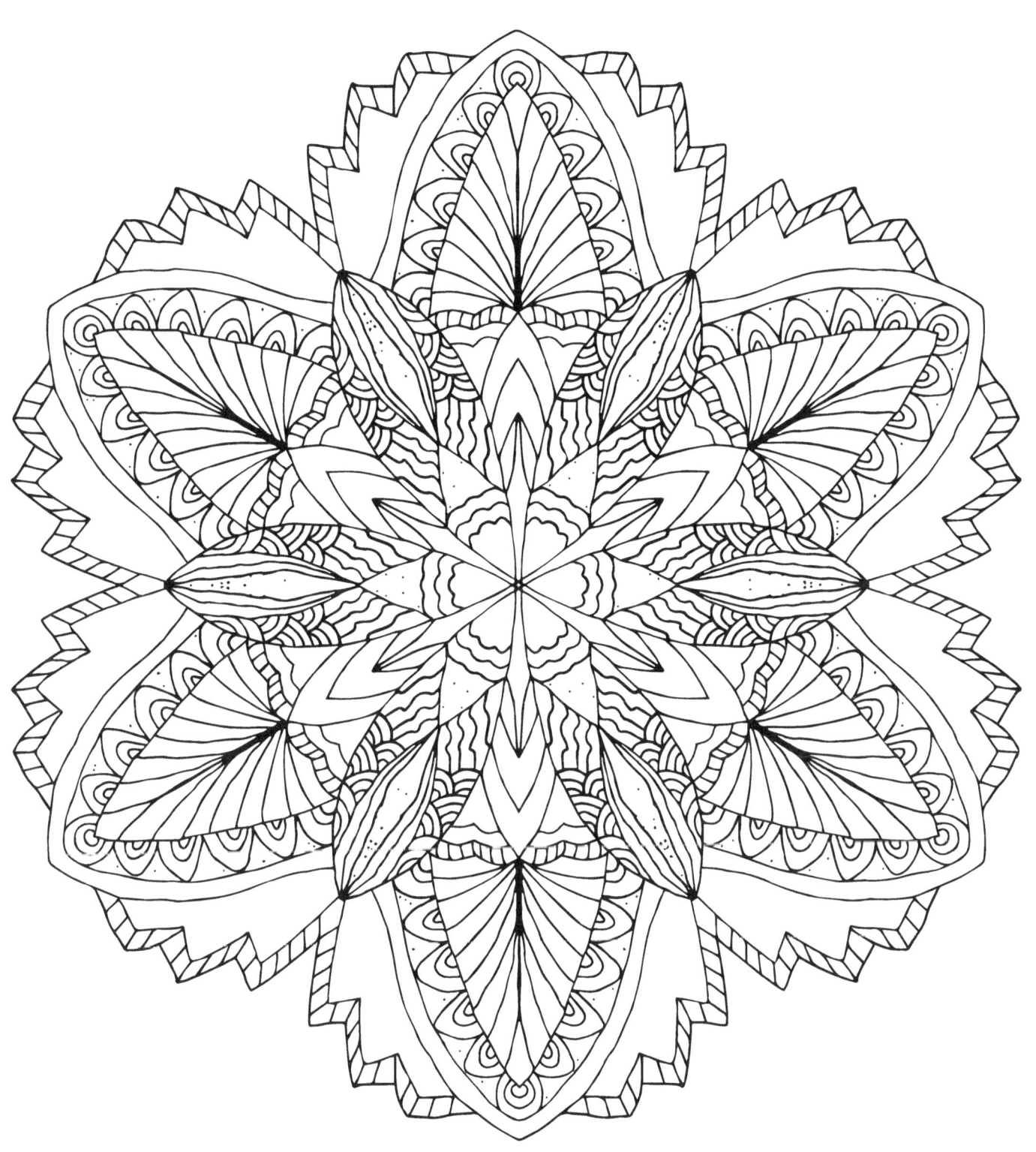

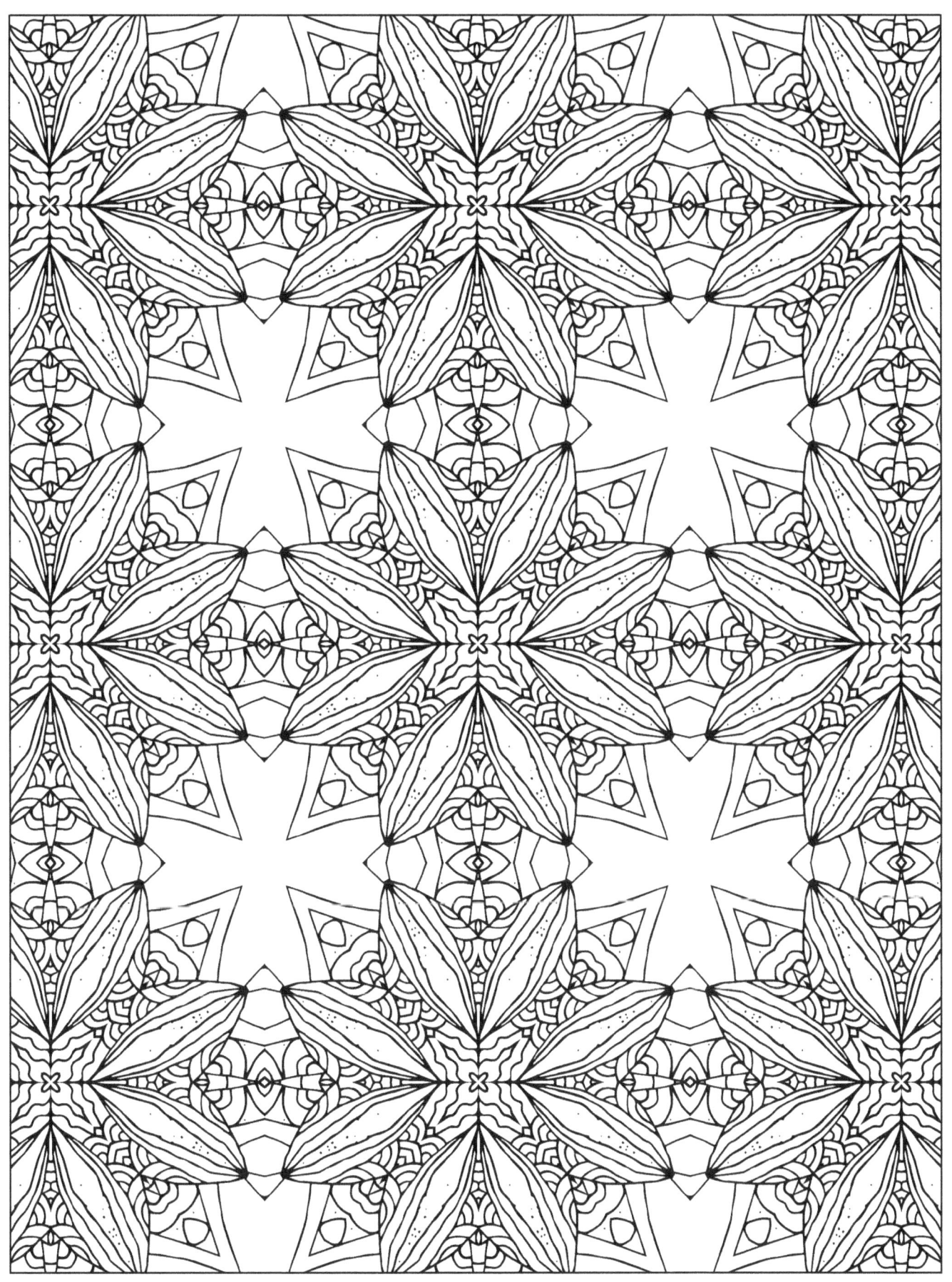

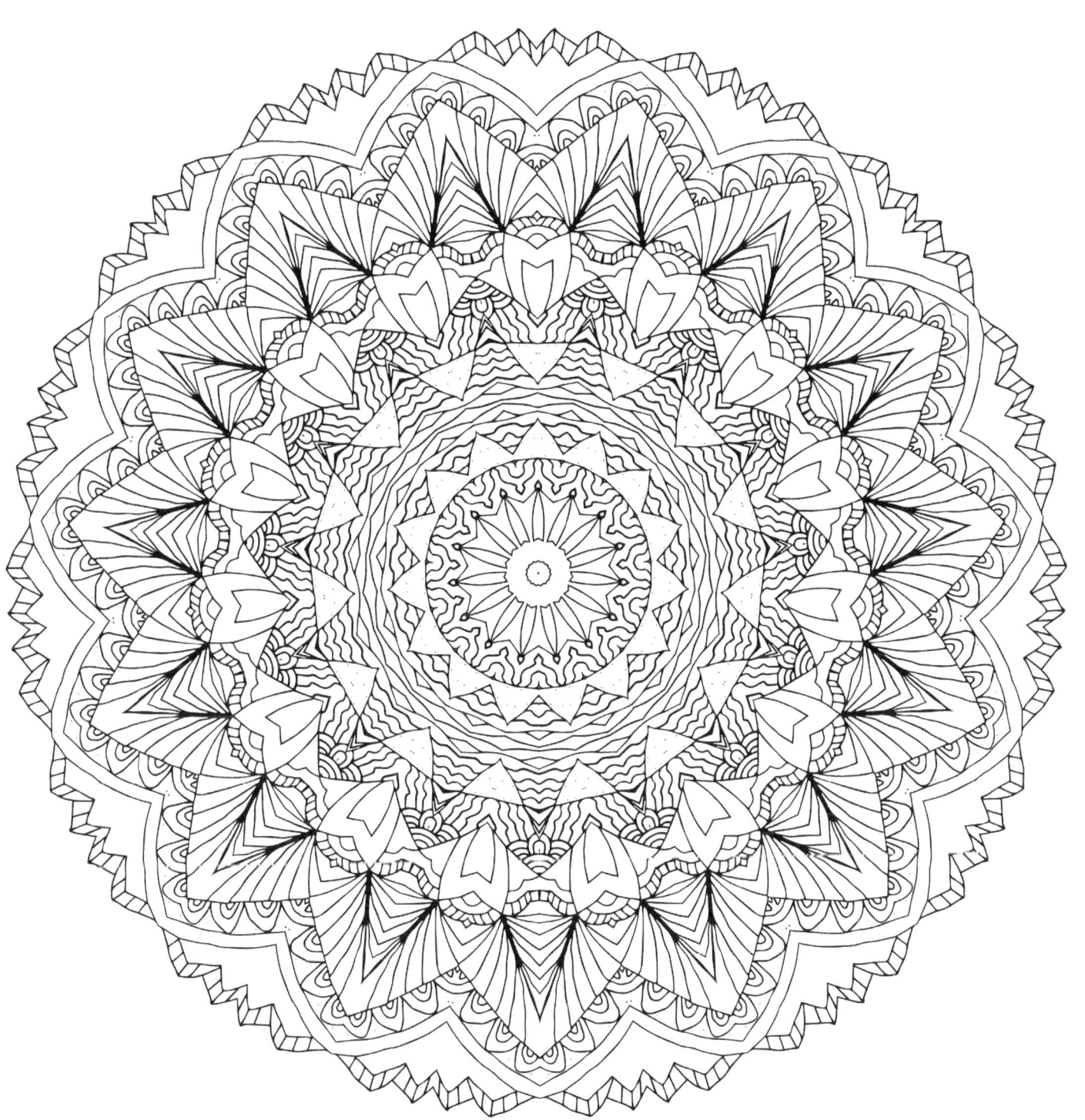

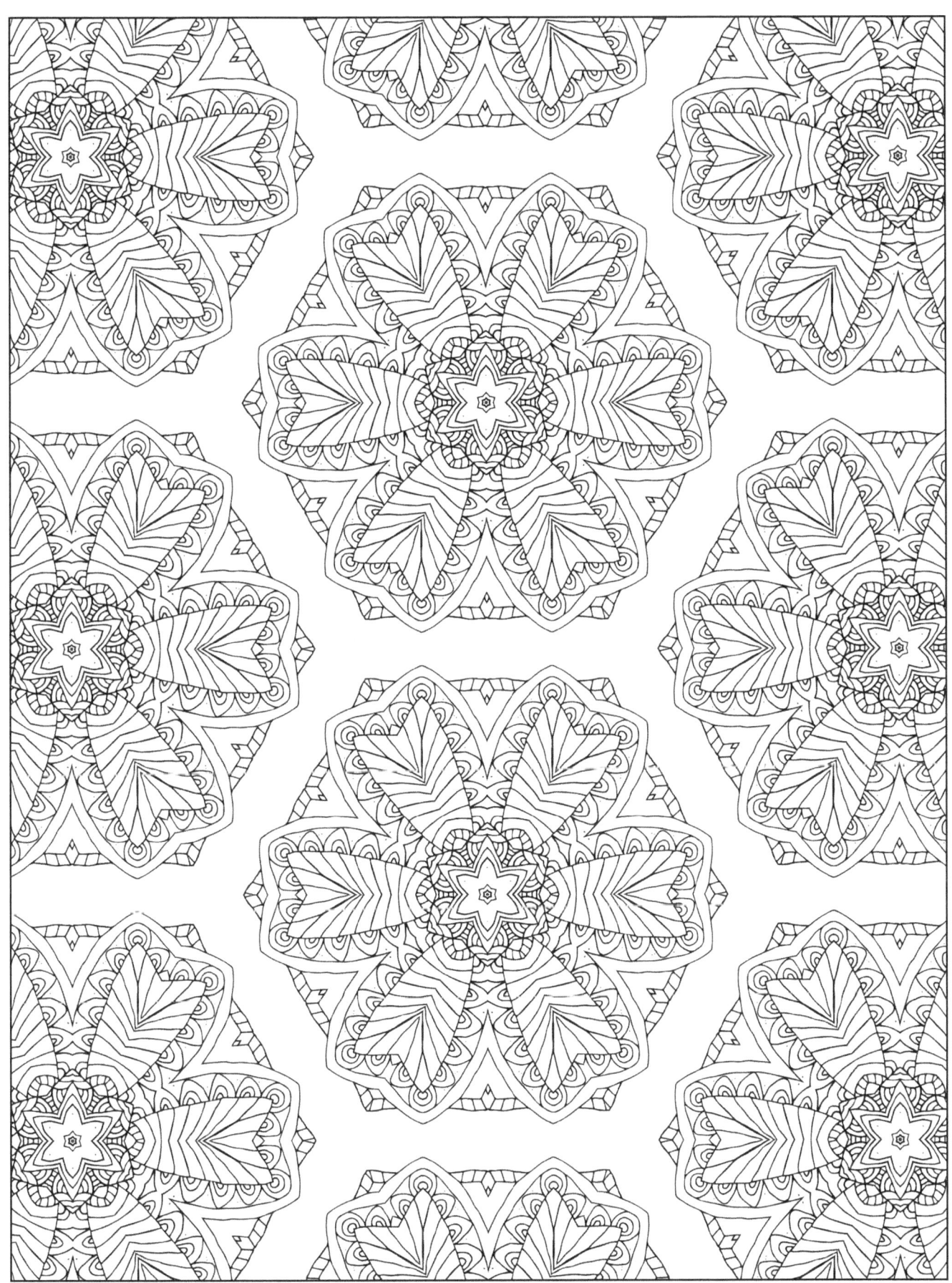

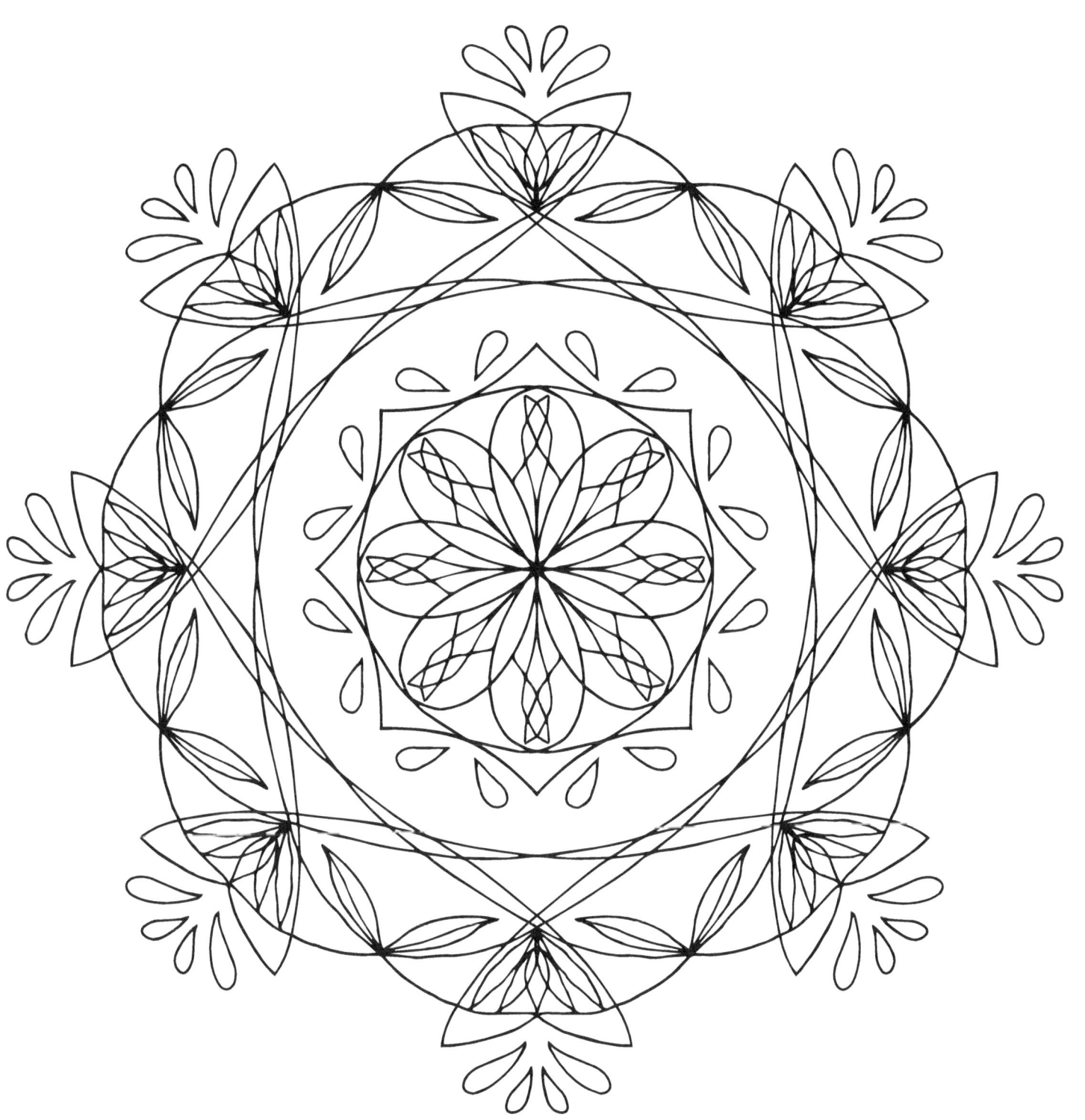

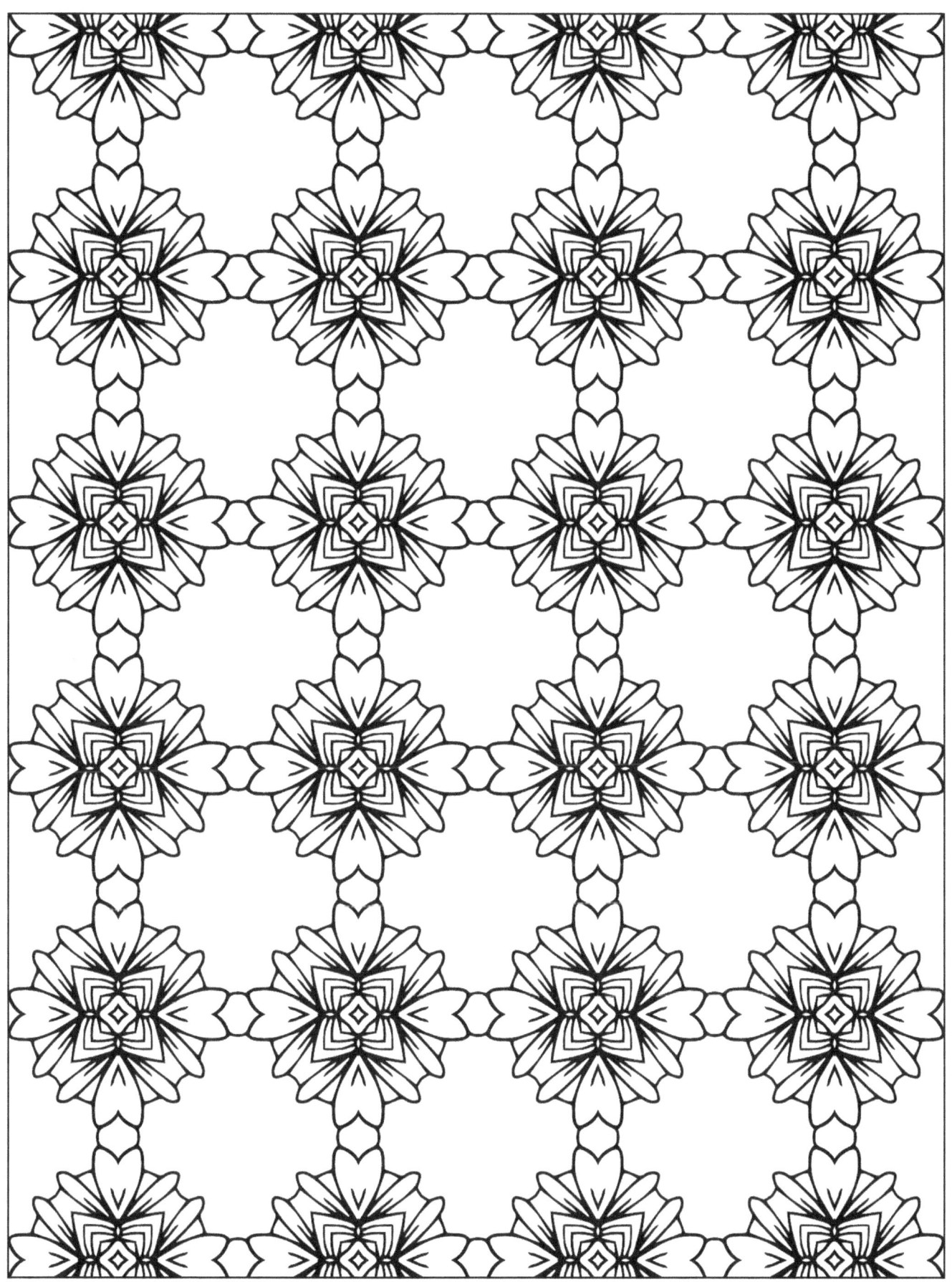

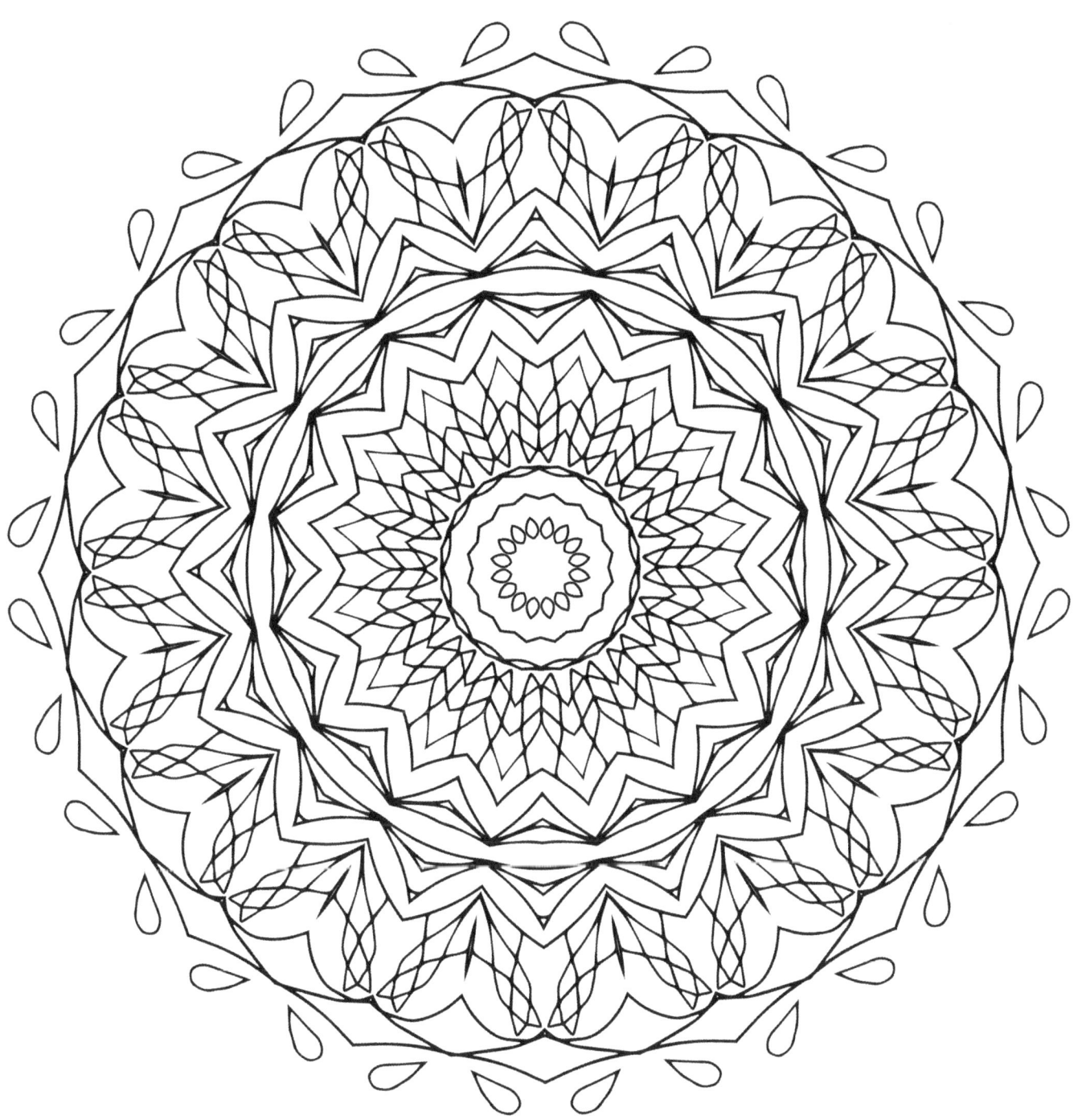

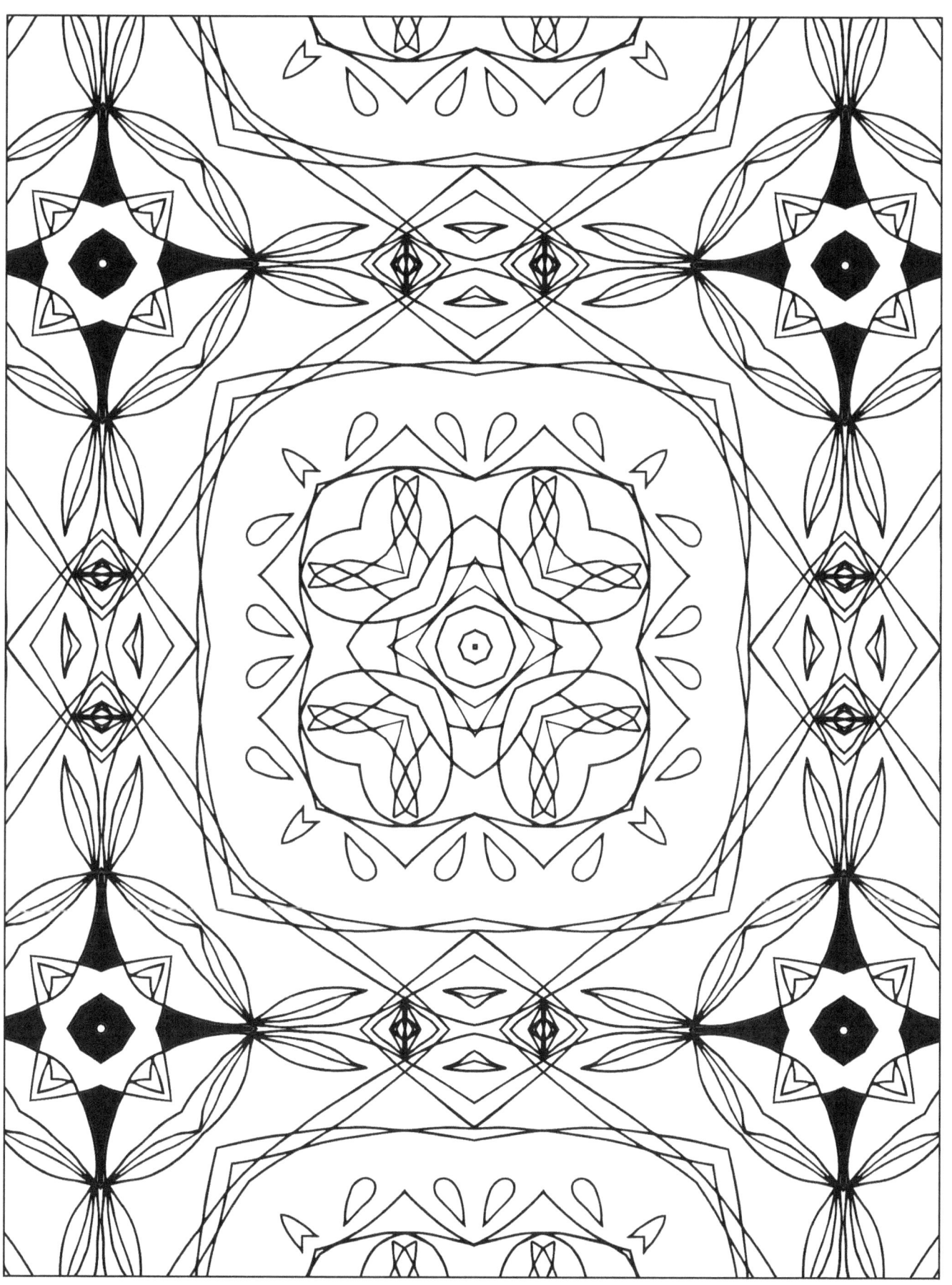

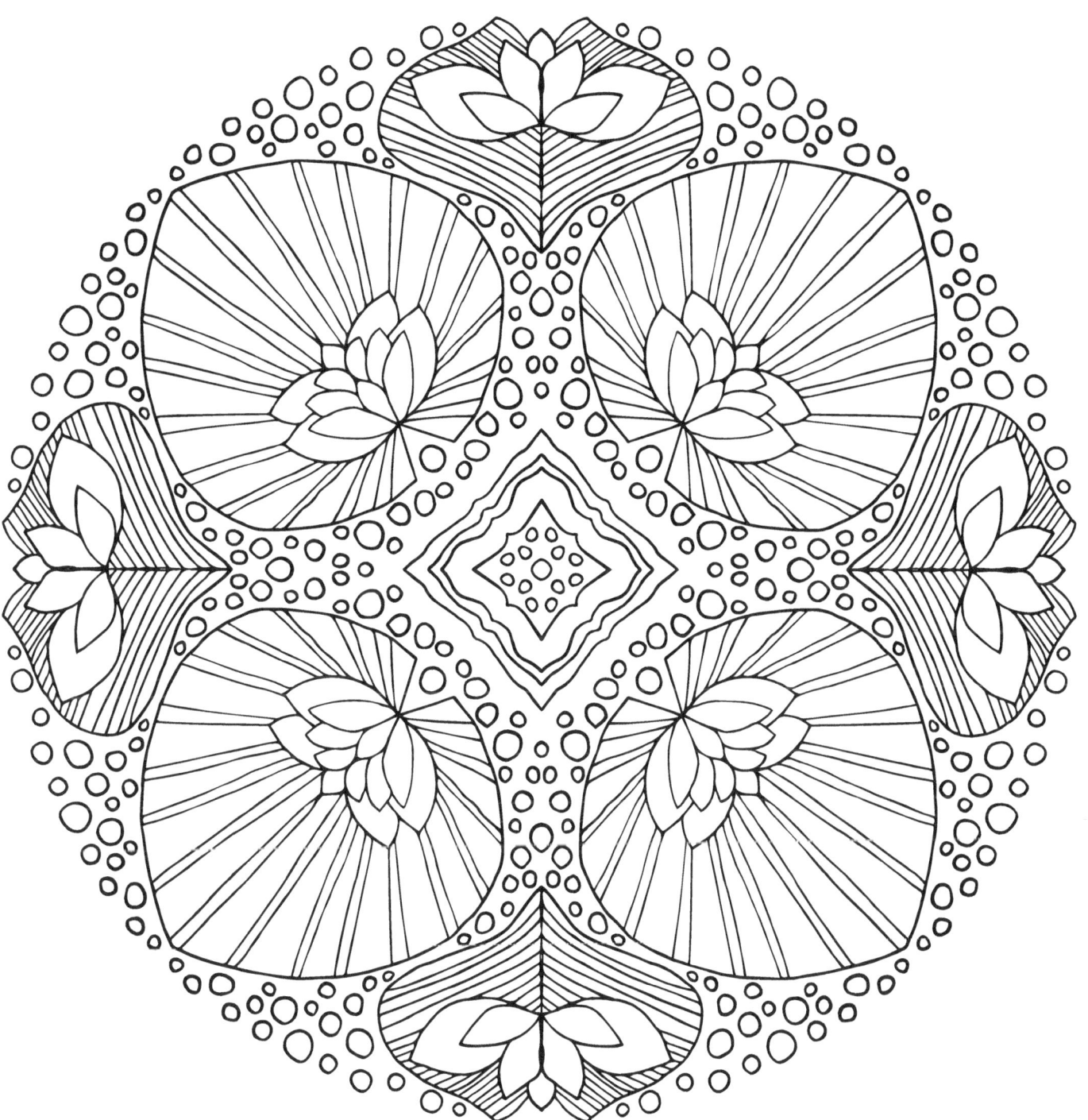

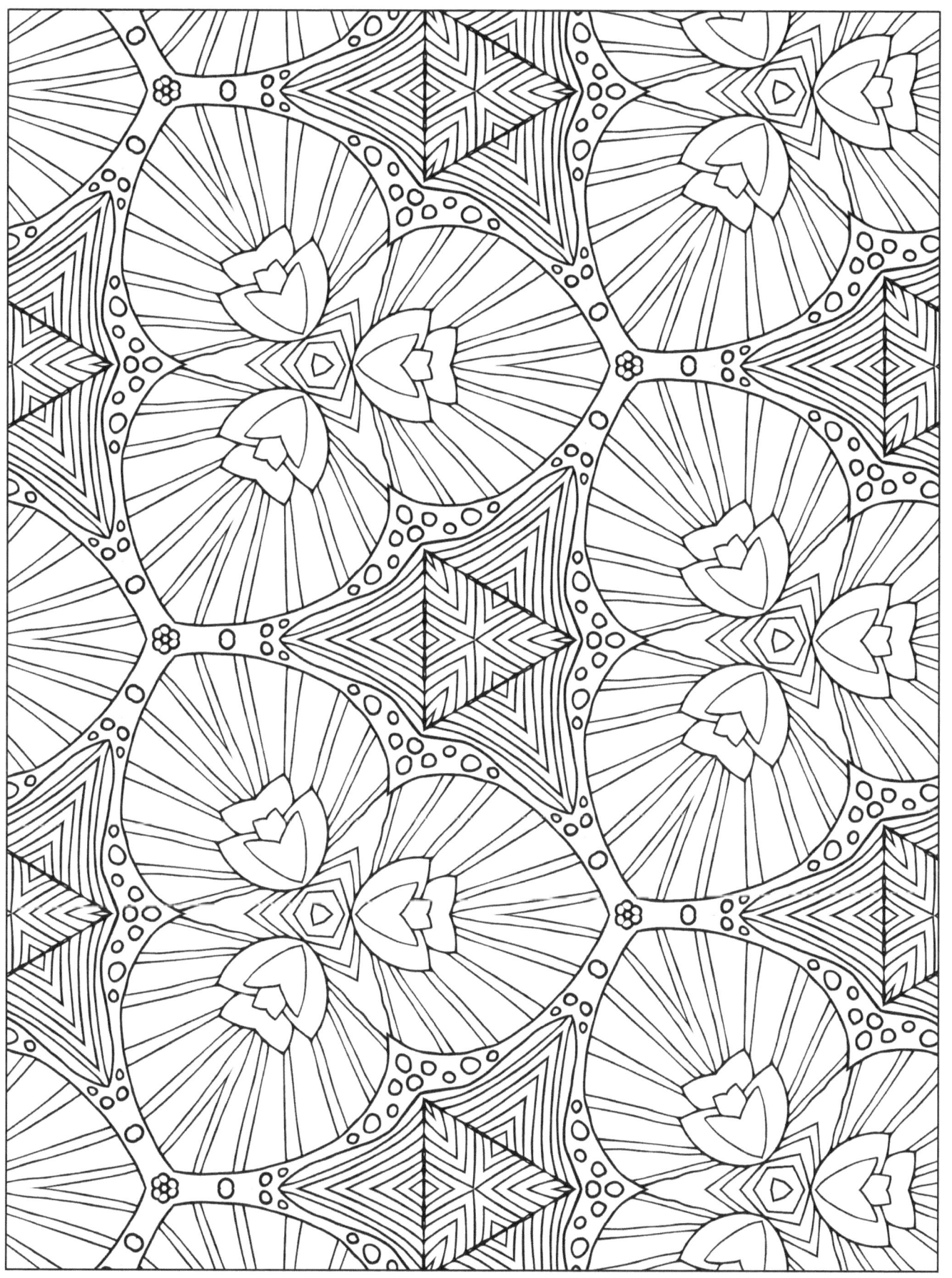

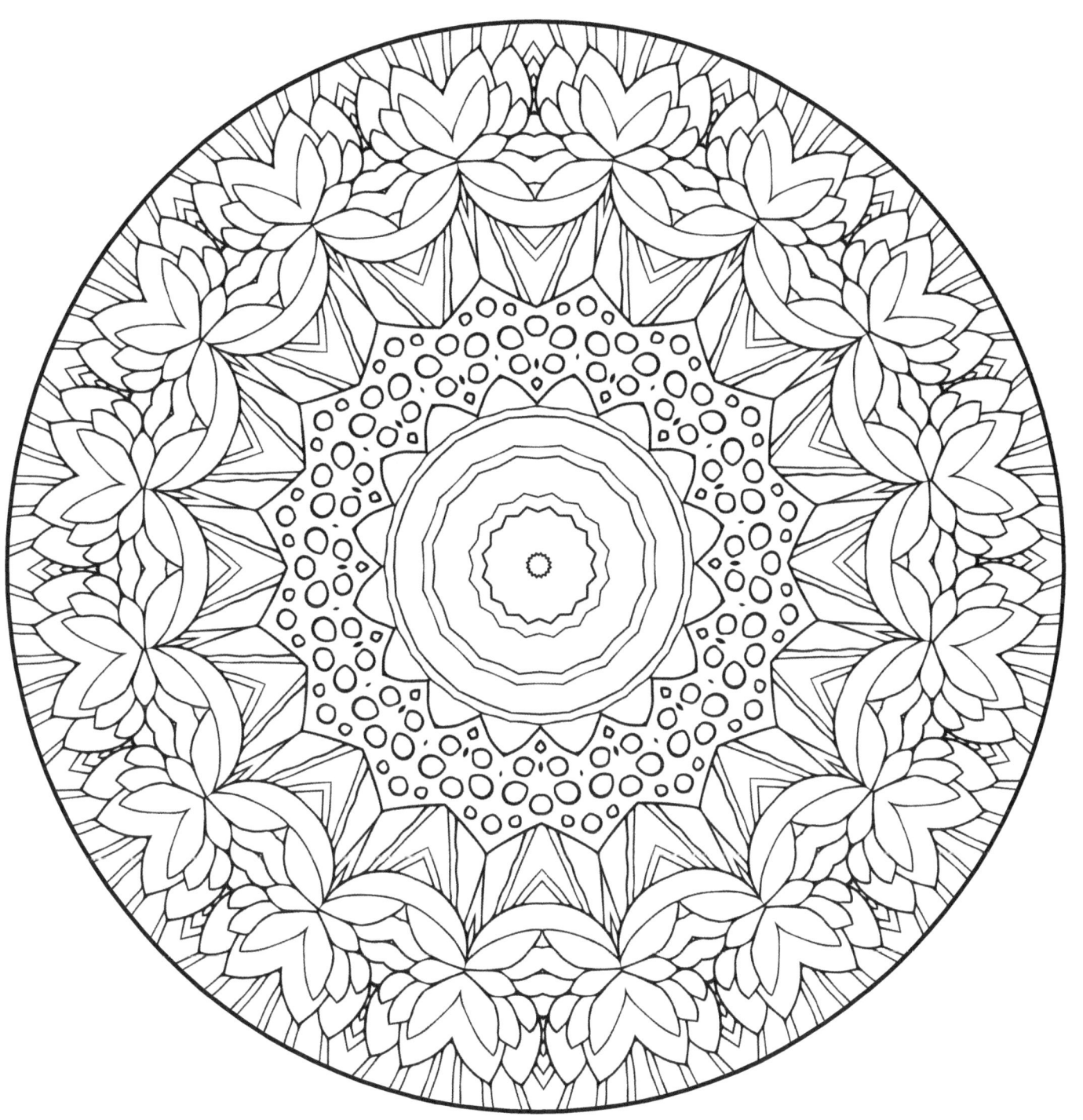

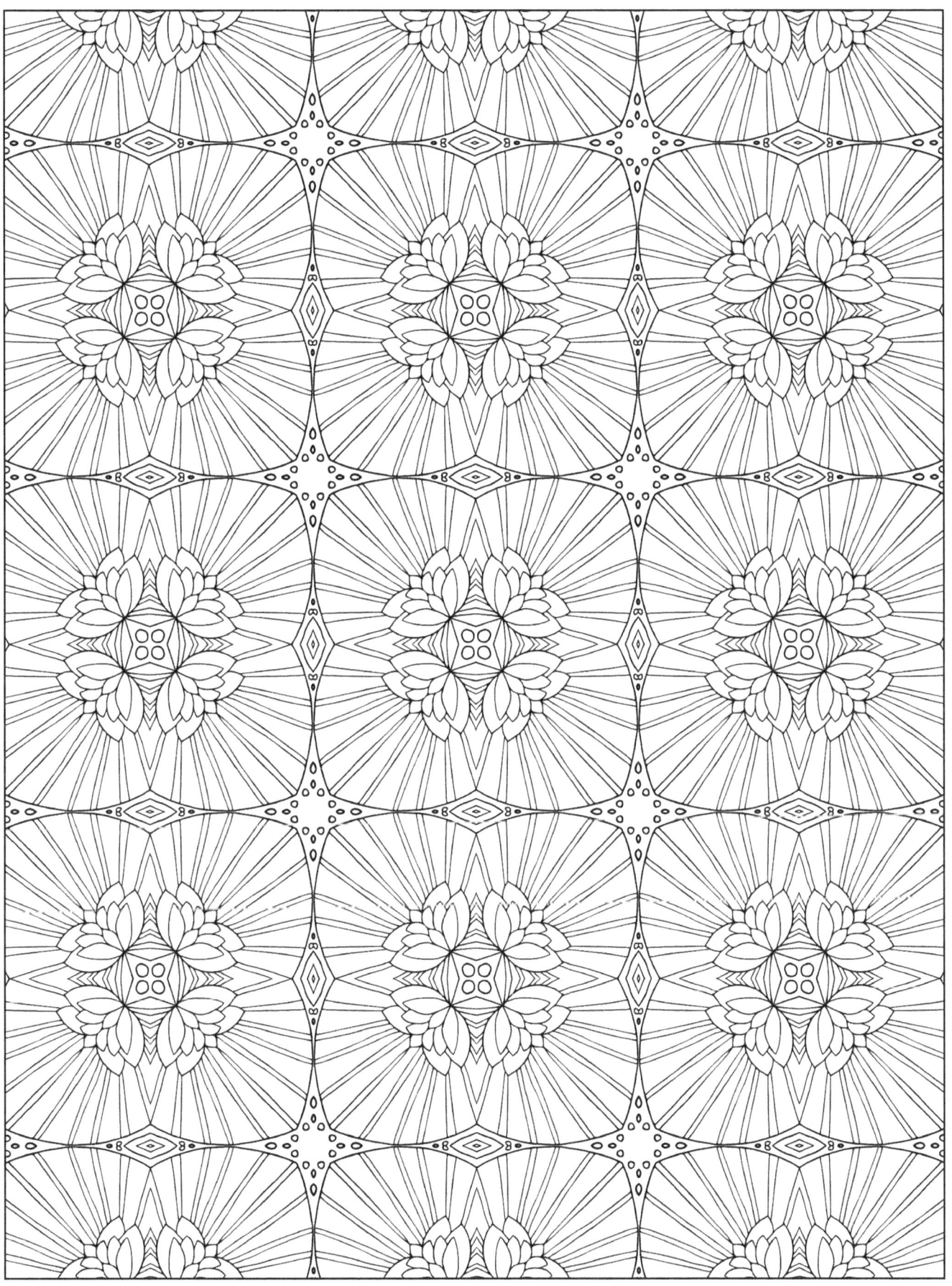

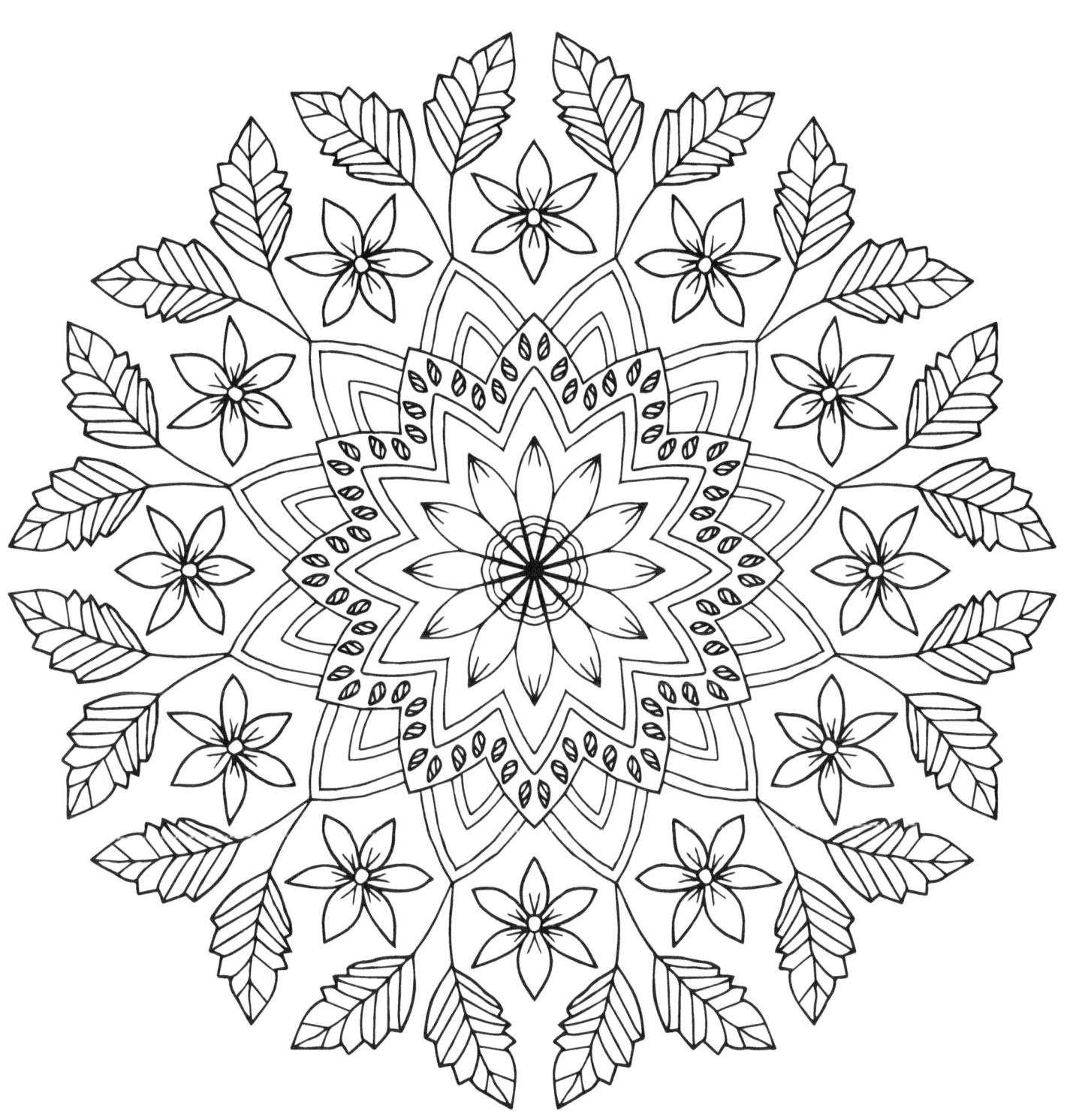

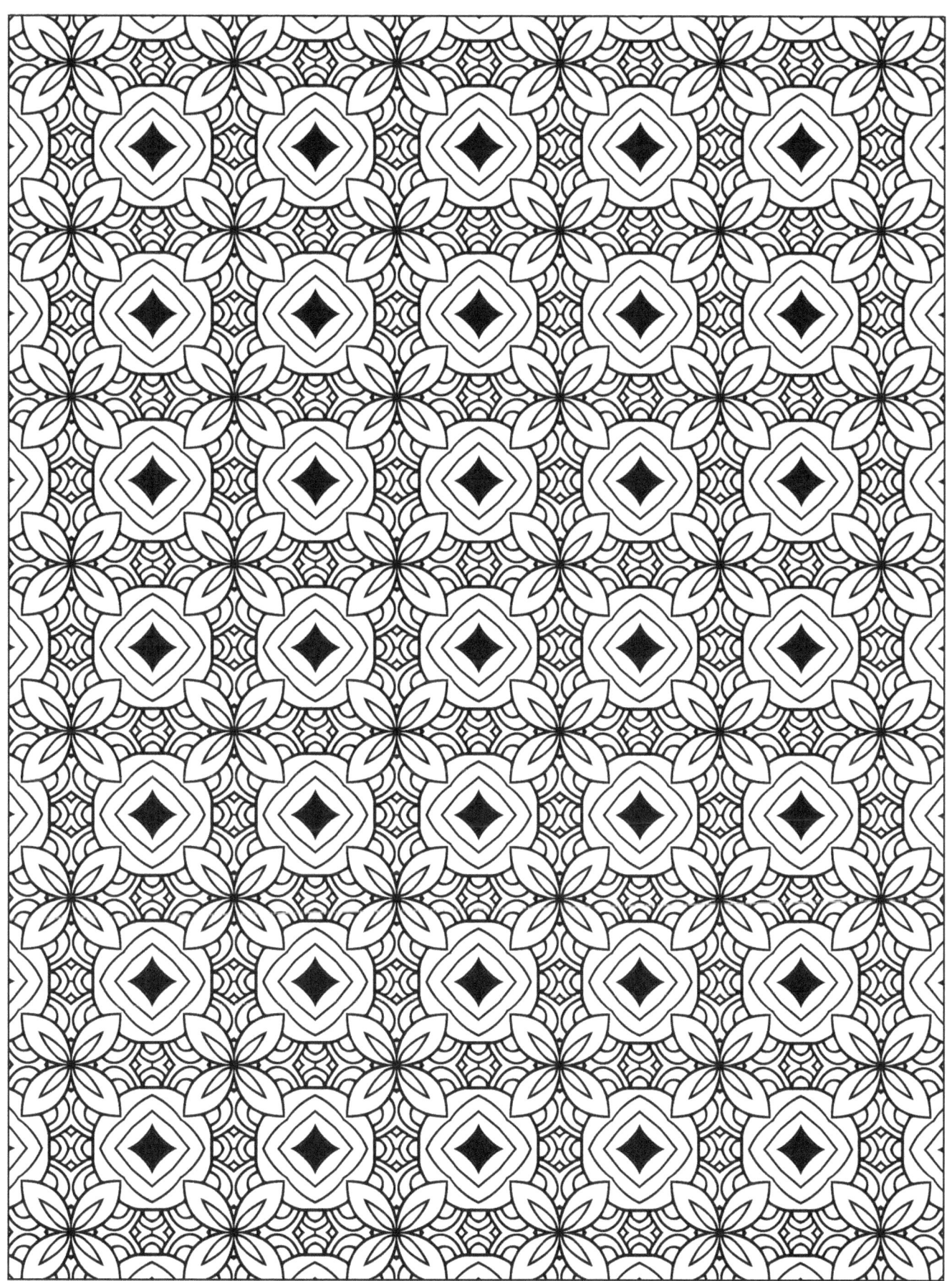

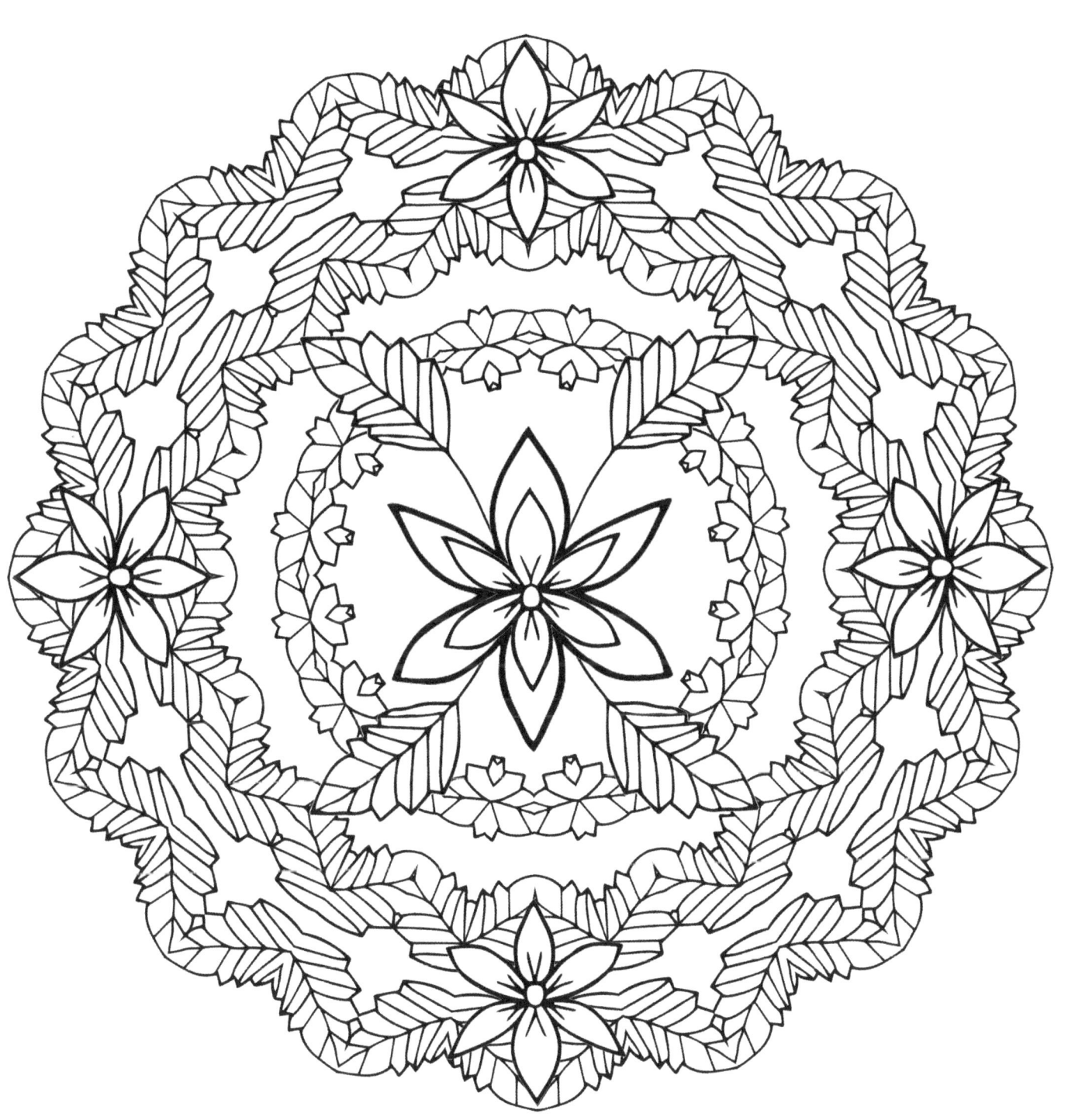

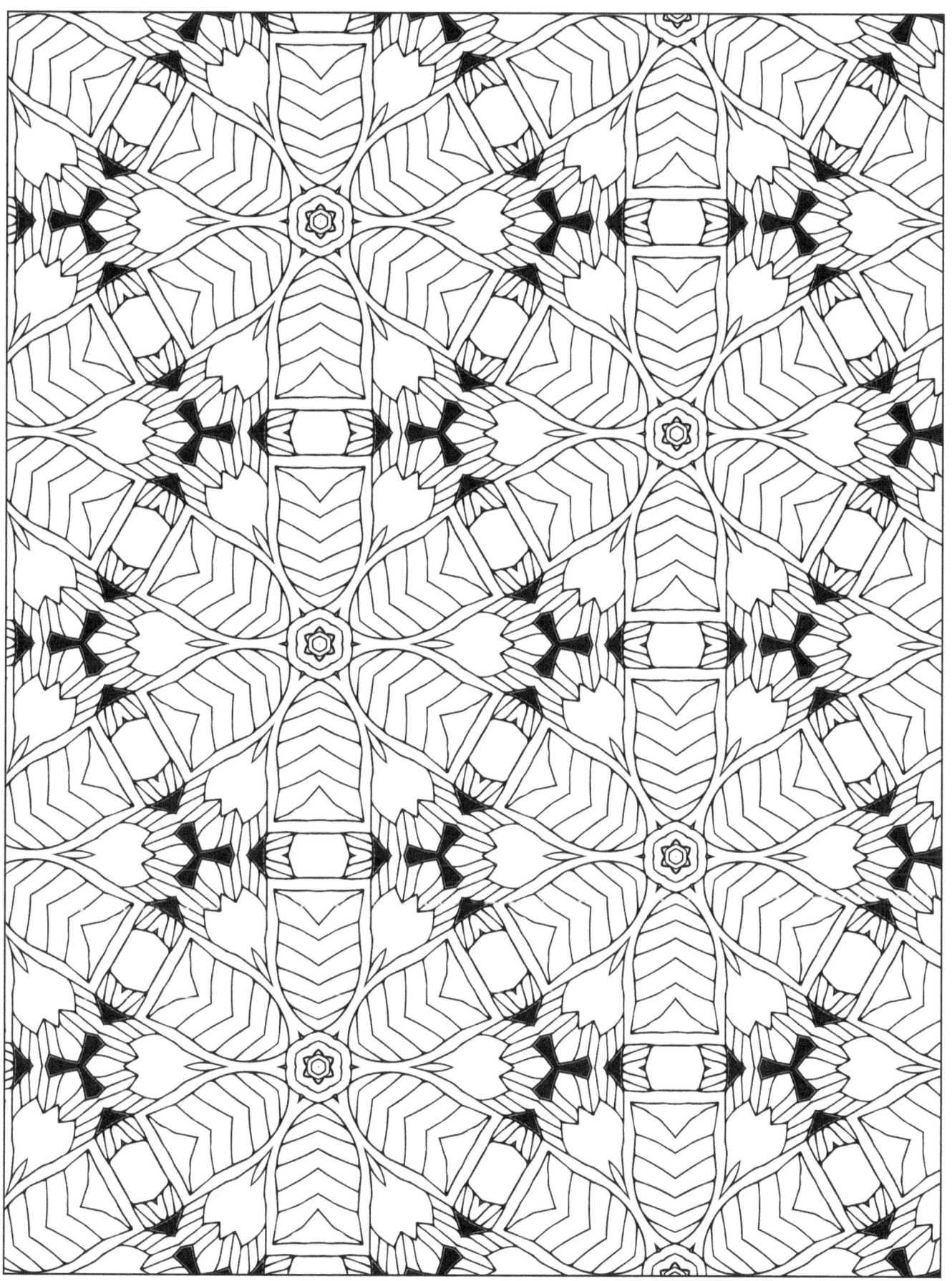

# COLOR TEST PAGE

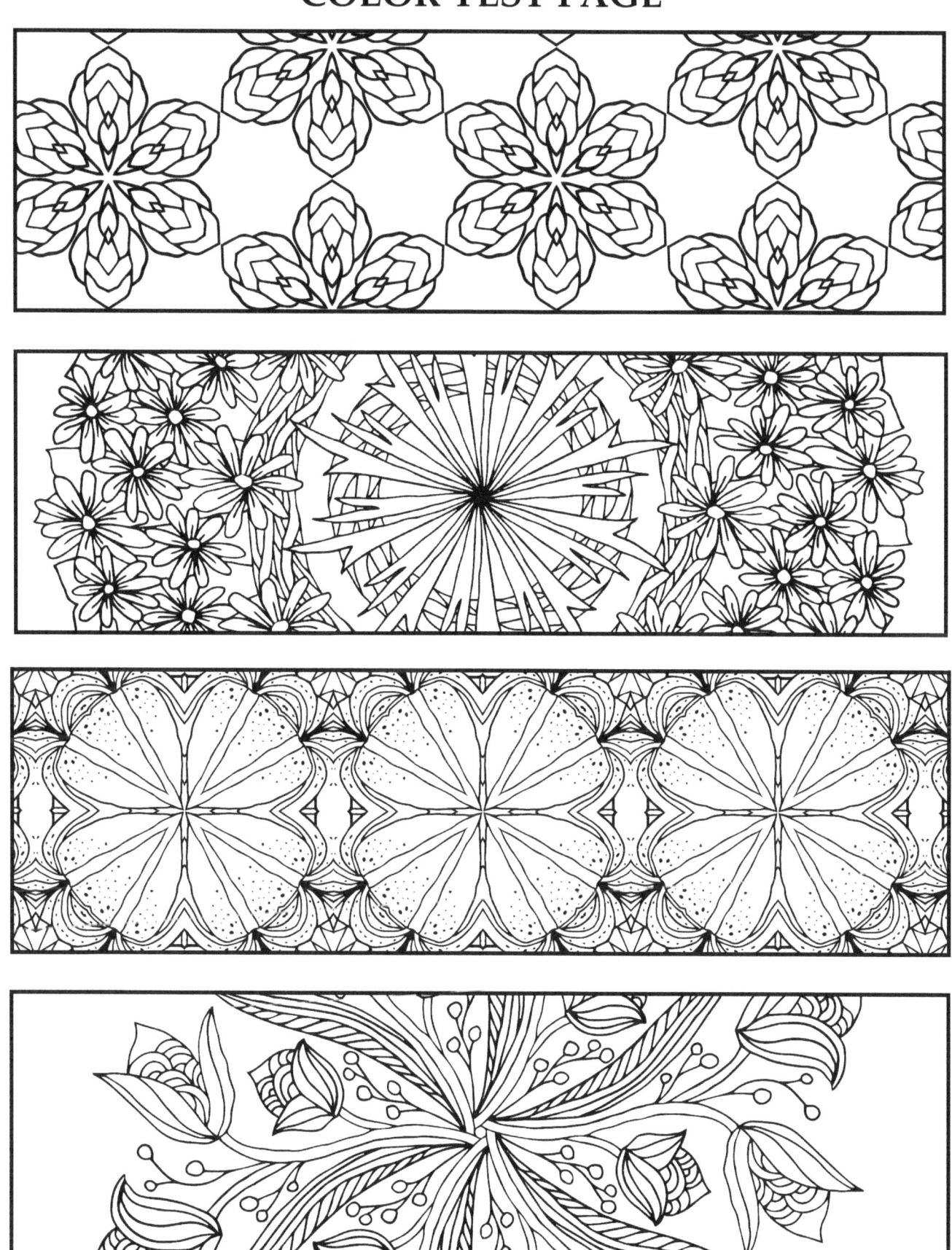